"Sheva Rajaee has written an important boo... the topic of relationship obsessive-compulsive disorder (ROCD). For anyone struggling with obsessive doubt about whether or not you're with 'the One,' this book offers information and tools to help you find more peace, freedom, and love."

—**Sheryl Paul**, author of *The Wisdom of Anxiety*
and *The Conscious Bride*

"Sheva Rajaee masterfully debunks the 'myth of the One,' which plagues individuals with ROCD, taking the reader through current research on the etiology, maintenance, and treatment of this increasingly problematic anxiety disorder. She provides sufferers with clear steps to confront their anxiety in the service of enhancing one's relationship satisfaction with demonstrable, meaningful, and lasting results."

—**Jayson L. Mystkowski, PhD, A-CBT**, founder, director, and
licensed clinical psychologist at Cognitive Behavior Health
Partners in Los Angeles, CA; and associate clinical professor
of psychology at the University of California, Los Angeles

"Sheva Rajaee masterfully dissects the 'myth of the One' while providing guidance on how to live in the uncertainty of a myth-free world. She explains the trickery of ROCD with the kind of empathy and understanding only possible through lived experience. This book will ignite your anxiety while teaching you how to control the flame. And we are all better off for it."

—**Allison Raskin**, podcaster, mental health advocate,
and best-selling coauthor of *I Hate Everyone But You*

"Reading *Relationship OCD* feels like talking with an intimate friend, a compassionate and knowledgeable therapist, a trusted confessor, and a loved partner all in one. Rajaee weaves together neuroscience, philosophy, and psychology to address some of the toughest issues in our private lives. Love and doubt, shame and longing, fear and hope—they're all in this highly readable book, and always with complete sensitivity and expert knowledge."

—**Eli R. Lebowitz,** associate professor in the Yale Child Study Center, and author of *Breaking Free of Child Anxiety and OCD*

"The condition of OCD has many subsets which continue to perplex the clinical population, as well as many mental health professionals. This book provides valuable information and guidelines for managing this extremely misunderstood facet of OCD. Many persons who might otherwise be misdiagnosed or misunderstood now have a resource to educate themselves and others about this illusive condition."

—**Steven Phillipson, PhD,** world-renowned expert in the treatment and understanding of OCD, and owner and clinical director of the Center for Cognitive-Behavioral Psychotherapy for twenty-five years

"A well-written, extremely practical step-by-step guide to overcoming ROCD. Sheva achieves the difficult task of combining cognitive behavioral therapy (CBT), acceptance and commitment therapy (ACT), and exposure therapy into a cohesive and easy-to-use approach. Highly recommended, both for those who suffer from ROCD and therapists who work with them."

—**Russ Harris**, author of *The Happiness Trap* and *ACT Made Simple*

# Relationship
# OCD

A CBT-BASED GUIDE
TO MOVE BEYOND
OBSESSIVE DOUBT, ANXIETY
& FEAR OF COMMITMENT
IN ROMANTIC RELATIONSHIPS

Sheva Rajaee, MFT

New Harbinger Publications, Inc.

## Publisher's Note

*This publication is designed to provide accurate and authoritative information in regard to the subject matter covered. It is sold with the understanding that the publisher is not engaged in rendering psychological, financial, legal, or other professional services. If expert assistance or counseling is needed, the services of a competent professional should be sought.*

No people named in this book reflect actual clients. The stories presented here are amalgamations.

Distributed in Canada by Raincoast Books

NEW HARBINGER PUBLICATIONS is a registered trademark of New Harbinger Publications, Inc.

Copyright © 2022 by Sheeva Rajaee
New Harbinger Publications, Inc.
5674 Shattuck Avenue
Oakland, CA 94609
www.newharbinger.com

Cover design by Amy Daniel; Acquired by Ryan Buresh; Edited by Brady Kahn

All Rights Reserved

---

## Library of Congress Cataloging-in-Publication Data

Names: Rajaee, Sheva, author.
Title: Relationship OCD : a CBT-based guide to move beyond obsessive doubt, anxiety, and fear of commitment in romantic relationships / by Sheva Rajaee.
Description: Oakland, CA : New Harbinger Publications, Inc., [2022] | Includes bibliographical references.
Identifiers: LCCN 2021036237 | ISBN 9781684037919 (trade paperback)
Subjects: LCSH: Commitment (Psychology) | Intimacy (Psychology) | Interpersonal relations | Anxiety. | Obsessive-compulsive disorder. | Cognitive-behavioral therapy.
Classification: LCC BF619 .R35 2022 | DDC 158.2--dc23
LC record available at https://lccn.loc.gov/2021036237

Printed in the United States of America

24     23     22

10     9     8     7     6     5     4     3     2

Without a shadow of a doubt,

For J.M.R.

# Contents

# Introduction

Lila, a thirty-year-old marketing director, is getting married in just two months. And so far, all she knows for certain is that she's absolutely terrified to take the next step. She nervously fidgets on the denim blue couch in my office as she wonders aloud, "Is it even fair to stand in front of him and his entire family and say yes when I'm having all these doubts? I mean, I'm just supposed to know, aren't I?" I resist the gnawing urge to jump in and try to save her from the pain she's feeling today, a pain I've seen hundreds of times before. Instead, I readjust in my chair and wait as she continues, "Of course, the hard part is that he's actually amazing. I've never been treated better in my entire life! We laugh all the time, share similar values, and really care about each other. He's exactly the kind of partner I would have hoped for. But I don't always have that *feeling*, you know what I mean?"

I know exactly what Lila means and, my guess is, so do you. She is about to make one of the biggest commitments of her life, and she would like to be absolutely certain that she isn't making a mistake. She would like to have that feeling, the one she was promised she would feel one day, an indicator she has found the right person. She would like to have reassurance that, in committing to this person, she won't ever feel regret or hurt or find herself falling in love with someone else. She would like certainty that, out of all the millions of options in the world, the person she has chosen will fulfill her, excite her, challenge her, and love her, no matter what, until the end of time. In short, Lila is asking me how she can possibly move forward when her reality doesn't match up with the love story she was promised.

We all know the story; it's practically imprinted on us since birth. Girl meets Boy (it's usually just that binary), and they have instant chemistry, an undeniable attraction. He's the man she always dreamed of, the dashing knight who takes away her pain and completes her so that she wants for nothing. She is his soul mate, the woman he's waited for all his life, who accepts him unconditionally and knows exactly what he needs without his ever needing to express it. Together, they live in perfect harmony, craving nothing and no one else in life because they have one another. Two perfect children and an impossibly large (and somehow affordable) home follow suit as they grow old together, nestled by the cozy fireside of their love. Boy and Girl have found "The One," their soul's counterpoint in another. We look on and think, "Those two figured it out! They really are the lucky ones…"

Now consider the thousands of ways you've been told this story, what we'll call the "Myth of the One." Have you ever heard it described as a myth, which honors some level of fantasy and untruth? More likely you understood it to be a fact of life. Consider then how you grew up to expect some version of this story in your adult relationships, and perhaps how disappointed you might have felt to discover it wasn't quite as easy as you had hoped it would be to find this particular brand of love. The Myth of the One, which I'll refer to in this book by the shorthand form MOTO, sounds like this: "If only you find the right one, the right person, all your pain and suffering will vanish, and you'll live happily ever after. You won't need to work too hard on your relationship, because it will feel natural and easy! You'll just know it when you feel it, and if you don't feel it, you're probably settling."

But that's just not true. And while real love is somewhat less glamorous, it is no less worthy. The actual process of loving another person takes willingness, patience, and plenty of hard work. Good relationships are hard to find and even harder to maintain, requiring herculean efforts of vulnerability, patience, and selflessness to thrive—they are not for the weak of heart, and they certainly don't just happen to us. To love fully, we must choose to lower our walls and resistances, allowing another person to see us, to see *all* of us, even the *I can't show these parts of me; they're ugly and unlovable* parts. Real love requires that we constantly evaluate and reevaluate our own blocks and insecurities and that we commit not only to the other but to a process of endless self-growth.

MOTO says that finding the right person is a straight shot to lifelong certainty and security, and healthy relationships certainly do offer some of this. But the truth is that real love requires a profound tolerance of uncertainty; it requires great risk and the willingness to walk forward even when you don't know what's up ahead and are terrified to find out. It's no wonder that Lila is having anxiety about her choice! She's about to take one of the most important and impactful risks of her life, and her anxious brain wants to be absolutely sure she's not making a huge mistake.

Lifetime commitment can give anyone cold feet, and it's normal to feel apprehension and anxiety when facing life's most important decisions. But for Lila and probably for you, this is no ordinary doubt. And the questions she's asking me about the rightness of her partnership aren't new; they've been explored before. In fact, it's easily the hundredth time Lila has asked some version of this same question in the last month alone. Almost every week, Lila comes to session with relentless doubts about the rightness of her partner and the trueness of her love. No matter how many times she has been reassured by friends and family members, and no matter how many times she has decided she loves her fiancé, Lila's brain still keeps asking that same painful, gnawing question *What if you're making the biggest mistake of your life?* The core of what Lila feels is universal: we all want certainty. But her need to acquire that certainty is not. Like you, she's begun to wonder if her doubts are more than just typical nerves.

Do these thoughts sound familiar? You know, the ones that pop up seemingly out of nowhere, asking hundreds of times per day, *What if they are the wrong person? Are we really compatible, or am I just settling?* or even *What if this is all a lie and I'm just duping myself into thinking this is true love?* Are these thoughts (painful enough on their own) accompanied by gut-wrenching anxiety, mental fog, panic, and maybe even aversion to your loved one's presence? If so, you might be struggling with more than just cold feet.

So you turn to your friends and family members hoping for clarity, but they hear your doubts and assume, "Maybe there isn't enough chemistry" or "They're just not the one. You'll know it when you feel it," and encourage you to break it off and move on. But breaking up doesn't feel quite right either! You find yourself stuck—unable to commit to more in the relationship because of your obsessive doubts, but also unwilling to leave. If you do decide to leave this person, or they decide to leave you, you don't feel any better. In fact, you might feel that leaving them was the real mistake. Sure, dating is confusing, and all breakups are hard, but this feels different. The temporary relief you feel at no longer experiencing intrusive thoughts is replaced with a new worry: *Did I just let my anxiety get the best of me?* Dazed and confused, you eventually move on to another relationship, only to see the same pattern. *There's no one out there for me,* you conclude, or maybe this is when you succumb to one of the most isolating phrases in the human experience: *I'm just not meant for love.*

Of course, not all breakups are caused by your anxiety, and there's no good reason to stay in a truly toxic partnership; none of the tools, principles, and theories in this book have been conceptualized for relationships where trust and respect have been eroded or destroyed. (If signs of verbal, physical, or sexual abuse exist in your relationship, don't read ahead. Instead, consider speaking to a mental health professional, as feeling doubt about abuse, toxicity, and dismissive or disrespectful behavior is a marker of psychological health, not an anxiety disorder.) But what if the problem isn't the person you're with or the connection you share? What if the problem is that you are experiencing a theme of obsessive-compulsive disorder (OCD) known as relationship OCD (ROCD), which affects hundreds of thousands of people per year and is much more an anxious way of thinking than a good reason to leave a loving partnership?

ROCD is a manifestation of anxiety marked by obsessive doubts about your relationship: whether you love your partner, whether your partner loves you, how attracted you are to your partner, how compatible you are, and, of course, if they are The One. These doubts occupy your mind, driving you to engage in compulsive behaviors like reassurance seeking, ruminating, and distancing yourself from your partner to avoid feeling triggered. Over time, these persistent doubts and compulsive behaviors can cause resentment, insecurity, and relationship disillusionment. What's worse, left untreated, your anxiety can keep you from ever having the good love you've hoped for. It can keep you isolated and alone while you endlessly seek to find the perfect person, the one who won't trigger your fears.

The possibility of having anxiety might be unsettling, but recognizing and addressing this is the starting point to profound healing. And if you have relationship anxiety or ROCD, you are in no way doomed to a lifetime of pain and lovelessness; there is a path forward. How do I know recovery is possible? Because years before I trained to become a therapist, I was embroiled in a battle with my own intrusive thoughts and crippled by the anxiety that came along with them. As a freshman at UCLA, I remember sitting in my dorm room late at night genuinely worrying that I was losing my mind because of the frequency and intensity of my intrusive thoughts, wondering how I could ever feel normal with a brain as loud and horrific as mine. Back then it was *What if I have cancer and I don't catch it in time?* But since those early days, my OCD has evolved to many other themes, including ROCD, all with the same underlying urgency to find the answer. I spent years seeking reassurance, drowning my pain in avoidance, and seeing therapist after therapist as I looked for the magical solution that would solve all my problems and put my mind at ease.

That perfect answer never came, but I found peace anyway.

Learning to manage and live with OCD, including ROCD, has been the most difficult, painful, and simultaneously beautiful experience in my life. It's been excruciating work, and I've made a lot of mistakes along the way. I've hurt people I love. I've had days when I have felt like the worst person in the world, like a horrible partner and a selfish friend— days when I felt decidedly undeserving of love. There have been other days when I've been overcome by the way my experiences have humbled and humanized me and by the way my suffering has transformed me for the better. My relationship with anxiety is complicated, but after years of work, I feel like I'm on the other side. What does this mean? It means that I live with OCD every single day, but it doesn't control my actions and it doesn't call the shots. Anxiety was with me the day I finished my graduate studies, and it was there the day I started private practice. It was there beside me at the altar a few years later, whispering in my ear as I gave my vows and looked into the eyes of the incredible person that I was choosing to share my life with. Most mornings I open my eyes and anxiety is already awake, bright-eyed and bushy-tailed, eagerly waiting to start the day with a fresh set of worries. I know my anxiety isn't going anywhere—it's part of who I am. But I have learned to coexist with it, to allow it a seat at the table, where it is present, but no longer interrupts the quality of my life.

As I became a therapist and then specialized in the treatment of anxiety disorders and OCD, I was shocked to see how little information was out there for those walking the same lonely path I was. I was shocked to see how hopeless some felt, when I knew and could see every day how possible meaningful recovery could be. In the decade I have spent specializing in the treatment of anxiety and OCD, hundreds of individuals have come to me desperate for an answer to what they feel is a crucial question, "Is my partner The One?" The thing is, I can never answer this question for my clients, and I can never answer this question for you. Life is filled with unanswerable questions, and simple answers simply won't work! Instead, you'll need to develop a strategy with far more lasting power than a onetime answer. You must learn to tolerate the uncertainty at the core of being human and at the heart of what it means to love. The truth is, no matter how hard your anxiety will try to convince you otherwise, you don't need to know if your partner is The One to have great love. You don't have to have all the answers to be happy.

In this book, I'll show you how to have a meaningful relationship without perfect answers. I'll show you what's causing your relationship anxiety, help you challenge faulty thinking, and develop the all-important mindset of willingness in the face of discomfort and doubt. Through this work, I'll aim to answer:

- What is relationship anxiety and how does it keep us in a worry loop?

- What tools and strategies can you implement to better manage your anxiety and grow connection and quality in your relationship?

- If you can't rely on the MOTO, then what kind of love story should you hope for?

The love you've always wanted is possible. It just might not look exactly like the story you've been sold. And to get there, you'll have to push through fear. You'll have to tear down your walls and retire your defenses. Because fear blocks attraction. It blocks intimacy and it blocks connection. Fear blocks love. If you want to find the love you seek, you will have to let go of fear and embrace uncertainty with open arms. You'll have to divorce MOTO and redefine altogether what good love looks and feels like—I'll show you how. Using research-backed interventions from the world of cognitive behavioral therapy (CBT), we'll start by challenging faulty assumptions about love, connection, and what relationships should be. Then, we'll utilize acceptance and commitment therapy (ACT) to expand your willingness to feel anxiety while still moving toward the values you hold and the kind of relationship you want. Finally, I'll show you how to harness the power of exposure and response prevention (ERP) to create healthier relationships, deeper intimacy, and, yes, less anxiety.

I've had the privilege of doing this work with thousands of clients and watched, as session after session, they have achieved lasting growth. I've watched clients struggle along the way and still keep climbing, and I have been honored to walk right beside them every step of the way. I've been emotional (let's be honest, cried) receiving updates from clients who've gone on to create the life they envisioned and the love they wanted, even after years of torturous intrusive thinking and anxiety. If it sounds like hard work to confront your ROCD thoughts and make peace with anxiety, let me tell you, it absolutely is. In fact, it might be one of the hardest things you'll ever do. But the very fact that you're here means there is something or someone worth fighting for: there's a reason to face your fears. After all, ROCD doesn't show up in just any relationship; it shows up in good ones, ones with lasting power, ones that might actually be worth doing the work for. And while MOTO says it should be effort-less, true-and-lasting love—the kind worth transforming for—doesn't come easily.

Rather, you'll come to see that love, the kind that heals and inspires us, is a daily habit. A habit of turning toward when you want to turn away, of staying open when all you want to do is run and hide, and of trusting you'll be okay even when there is no clear path forward. You'll come to see that love, in words attributed to relationship philosopher Erich Fromm, "isn't something natural. Rather it requires discipline, concentration, patience, faith, and the overcoming of narcissism. It isn't a feeling, it is a practice."

Let's get started.

# PART 1

# The Myth
# of the One

# CHAPTER 1

# The Anxious Spiral

This is a book about relationships and a book about anxiety. In fact, this book is as much about your relationship to anxiety as it is a guide to more fulfilling relationships. Whether through nature, nurture, or a combination of both, your anxious brain has decided that relationships, commitment, and love are dangerous. It has decided that the only way to mitigate the risk involved in loving another person is to warn you of all the possible downsides 24 hours a day, 7 days a week, 365 days a year (anxiety doesn't take vacation time). So while you spend hours debating whether you love your partner enough, whether they love you enough, or whether you're making the biggest mistake of your life in committing to them, your anxiety wins—it keeps you safe by keeping you separated. And while it may be tempting to jump right in and talk about how to feel more connected to your real-life partner, we've got to understand anxiety first. We've got to start as any good couples therapist managing an argument would, by illuminating the dynamics at play not just in your real-life relationship but in your relationship to anxiety. Because the fight you've been waging on anxiety, all the ways you've been trying to solve, escape, or avoid it, is keeping you from the very thing you want most: to love and to be loved.

I know that if you've picked up this book, it's probably because you want to feel more connected to your partner. You want to feel more love, fulfillment, attraction, and desire, and you have a hunch that your anxiety is standing in the way. Perhaps you've already attempted to solve the burning questions on your own and have spent hours, months, or even years trying to negotiate a peace deal with the painful voice in your head, the one that spews doubt and *what-if* horror stories on a 24/7 loop.

Usually by the time someone has looked up "relationship anxiety" or "ROCD," or has found their way into my office for treatment, they've realized that all the fighting and solving hasn't given them what they wanted; their anxiety hasn't gone away. In fact, they, like you, might feel more confused and filled with doubt than ever!

Don't get me wrong, I completely understand why you would be up in arms. Anxiety doesn't exactly make it easy to peacefully coexist. Rather, it poses thousands of questions and sends a barrage of doubt and discomfort your way, making it all but impossible to lay down your weapons and play nice. So you try to solve—or answer—the burning questions and find relief. Except, attempting to solve chronic doubt is the exact wrong thing to do: it gets you in trouble and keeps your anxiety alive and well.

*Wait, I'm not supposed to figure out if I truly love my partner? Or if they truly love me? Or if I'm making the right choice?*

That's exactly right! Seeking certainty breeds more uncertainty.

Like a finger-trap toy that gets tighter as you pull, the real answer is to accept no answer at all. And if this sounds confusing and counterintuitive, that's exactly the point. Fighting and solving away your anxiety hasn't worked, and it's time to try something entirely different. Now you might be wondering, *But how can I move forward without knowing the answer to these important questions?* I completely understand your concern. It's hard not to want answers when the thoughts forcing their way into your head are terrifying, painful, and even cruel at times. It's hard not to get caught up trying to solve away the questions anxiety poses—when they are incessant and accompanied by painful physical sensations that wrench your gut, fog your mind, and pull you out of the present moment— when they demand to be heard. That's the tricky thing: your anxiety is an expert at getting your attention. It knows exactly what to say to elicit a response and shows up with a terrifying sense of urgency. It's no wonder you've been fighting so much! This experience is truly painful. Just like the finger-trap toy, the way out is to relax into the feeling you've been trying to avoid for so long, and allow anxiety to release its grip on you, all on its own. To make peace with the nagging voice in your mind and make space for the discomfort it causes; to give up the fight.

That's a tall order, but brokering a peace deal might seem a little easier when we remember that anxiety isn't some evil curse sent to destroy our life. In fact, every single person you know has anxiety; they just experience it in varying degrees. Every single person you know has a dark and sometimes taboo voice in their head that whispers things like *What if you push that person into the street right now?* or *You glanced at that baby's bottom when you were changing her diaper. Are you some sort of pervert?* The difference is that for most people these thoughts come and go like odd little clouds in an otherwise blue sky, while in the highly anxious or obsessive mind they get stuck. They run on a constant loop that, left untreated, can wreak havoc on our quality of life and relationships.

Anxiety feels like:

- Racing thoughts

- Increased heart rate

- Tightness in the chest

- Rapid, shallow breathing

- Mental fog

- Gastrointestinal discomfort

- A sense of impending danger or doom

Although it feels uncomfortable, anxiety itself is not the problem. In fact, you need your anxiety, and if you could somehow wave a magic wand and rid yourself of it, you probably wouldn't survive too long.

The fascinating case of "the woman with no fear" illustrates exactly this point. In 1994, a group of researchers identified SM, a woman now in her fifties, who seemed to be unable to feel fear. It was discovered that SM had Urbach-Wiethe disease, an incredibly rare condition which causes calcium deposits to form in the brain. In her case, they formed over the amygdala, the very portion of the brain responsible for registering threat and producing a fear response in the body. They found that while SM could feel joy, sadness, anger, and frustration, she could not feel fear and had no anxiety whatsoever! And while on your worst days this may sound like a joyful reality, multiple accounts of SM's life show that her inability to register threat made her especially vulnerable to danger. For example, SM reported feeling no trepidation when handling poisonous spiders or snakes, though she originally reported disliking them. She shared that she had been held at gunpoint and knifepoint on multiple occasions and that she struggled to register appropriate personal boundaries, often standing nose to nose with complete strangers (Yong 2010). A researcher studying SM at the University of Iowa noted that her behavior continually led her back to the exact situations she should have been avoiding—and that this revealed how crucial the amygdala is in keeping us alive. Without the amygdala, we don't know how to stay away from danger; there's an evolutionary value to fear, and the amygdala is key to preserving that value (Adolphs et al. 1994).

Nope, there's absolutely nothing wrong with anxiety! In fact, as the research noted, your anxiety has significant evolutionary value—that is, as long as it's in the right proportions, as long as that vigilance is proportional to the level of threat around you. Being anxious isn't the problem. It's when undesirable but tolerable outcomes start to feel ten-out-of-ten dangerous that we begin to edge into what we call an anxiety disorder; when our brain's natural and healthy distress signal, the one that keeps us from getting too close to strangers or handling poisonous snakes, becomes so loud, irrational, and incessant that it threatens to paralyze us altogether. Urbach-Wiethe disease completely shut down SM's amygdala, the fear center of her brain. But what exactly is the role of the amygdala in your own experience of anxiety?

## The Neurobiology of Anxiety Disorders

Sometimes, as is the case with anxiety disorders, a helpful adaptation can go too far. And conditions like panic disorder, generalized anxiety

disorder, obsessive-compulsive disorder, and post-traumatic stress disorder (PTSD) are exactly that—they are the result of overactivity in an
almond-shaped cluster of neurons called the *amygdala*. Located at the
base of the brain in the oldest and most primitive region, the amygdala
receives input from our senses (sight, smell, touch) and processes this
information completely outside our awareness. When functioning correctly, the amygdala scans the environment and decides whether to
trigger a threat response (fight, flight, or freeze) or give the all-clear
signal to the brain to "Move along, nothing to see here!" It's the amygdala that fires up when we hear a rustling in the bushes and notice our
focus narrowing or when we see a stranger coming toward us late at
night and feel our heart rate increase at the possibility of impending
danger. And while SM's disease turned off her amygdala, leaving her
dangerously fearless, those with anxiety disorders lie at the other end of
the spectrum. The amygdala becomes overly attuned to threat, creating
or enhancing the possibility of danger when there isn't much at all.

Ideally, we'd like to experience a proportional threat response, to
accurately register the difference between real danger (in your relationship or otherwise) and the horror stories that keep us on edge. Why
then, do some people have a hyperactive amygdala while others view
threat more rationally? The answer, like so many things in the world of
psychology, is a mixture of genetics and upbringing, of nature and
nurture. Think of it like this: if you feel like you might be on the higher
end of the anxiety spectrum or could qualify for an anxiety disorder, it's
likely that the anxiety gene exists somewhere in your family line. Maybe
you have a parent with undiagnosed panic disorder or an aunt who experiences obsessive-compulsive tendencies. Studies have shown that
anxiety disorders are often inherited through family lines (Nestadt,
Grados, and Samuels 2010), but don't let that scare you, because the
prognosis for treatment is highly positive. That means, despite how
debilitating your anxiety feels, with the right kind of treatment and the
willingness to change, most people feel better. And so can you.

We'll explore exactly how nurture affects anxiety in the next chapter.
But for now, just know that the amygdala can also become sensitized

through environment, most notably through how safe or unsafe we felt as children and how our caregivers managed their own fears and anxieties. And while everyone's neurobiology develops in unique ways, the good news is that there is a treatment strategy aimed at calming a sensitive amygdala. The work in this book will help you do just that—scale back your anxiety through the application of tools that shift your relationship to discomfort. And while it might sound like pretty heavy lifting for a self-help book, healing a sensitive amygdala is entirely possible. In fact, multiple studies on the use of CBT and exposure and response prevention for anxiety and OCD have shown that these interventions can actually correct amygdala hyperactivity. That's right! You can do brain surgery simply by changing your behavior, just by applying the tools and techniques in the following chapters. And I'm not talking about years of intensive psychotherapy, because these same studies have found that brain change begins to occur *just two weeks* after the application of ERP, and these positive results last well after therapy has ended (Goossens et al. 2007).

Exciting news, right? You get to be the surgeon your parents always hoped you would be! I'm kidding, of course, but as a therapist who uses ERP with clients every single day, I know it works. I've seen the results firsthand. And while it's not helpful to assume that you'll completely overcome ROCD and relationship anxiety in a matter of weeks (the ERP studies just mentioned involved hours of daily exposure for multiple days on end), you do have the power to alter your reality. Through changes in your behavior, you can rewire your brain and see the world and your relationship through clearer eyes.

## Relationship Anxiety vs. ROCD

We'll discuss a little later in this chapter exactly how changing your behavior can soothe a sensitive amygdala, but first let's clarify an important bit of semantics. In this book, you'll hear me use the terms relationship anxiety (RA) and relationship OCD. So what's the difference? Essentially, it comes down to what label you feel best describes your experience and whether or not you qualify for an OCD diagnosis. The reason a therapist might say you have relationship anxiety rather than ROCD could be the severity of symptoms or level of impairment you may be exhibiting, with relationship anxiety being on the less severe end of the anxiety spectrum and ROCD on the more severe end. I've also known therapists who prefer to describe what's going on as relationship anxiety because they don't believe in diagnosis or labels. You might personally choose to use the term RA because explaining it to others feels easier than getting into the nuances of what it means to have OCD, if you do indeed qualify for that diagnosis.

But for the purposes of building a stronger relationship and better connection to your partner, it really doesn't matter which term you use. There are obsessions in both RA and ROCD, and there are compulsions in both. Both cause relationship dissatisfaction and contribute to a buildup of shame and depression if left untreated. Both can be devastating to your quality of life. The good news is that the treatment of RA and ROCD is identical, and while the strategies in this book will be framed through an OCD lens, everything you learn will apply whether what you're experiencing is better described as RA or ROCD. If you are curious to see if you qualify for a formal diagnosis of OCD, consider meeting with a mental health professional who specializes in the treatment of OCD and anxiety disorders. I've included resources for the right kind of help at the back of this book.

Up to now, we've covered our bases on what anxiety is and the role of the powerful almond-shaped fear center in your brain, the amygdala. But what exactly does it mean to have OCD, and how can understanding the building blocks of this anxiety disorder set you up for the kind of relationship and connection you always hoped to have?

## Understanding Obsessive-Compulsive Disorder

Often, the anxiety I see in my office has reached a level of severity that warrants a diagnosis of OCD, a psychiatric condition characterized by repetitive, intrusive, and distressing thoughts, images, and impulses called *obsessions*. These obsessions create significant anxiety and discomfort, and any behavior aimed at neutralizing obsessions, whether they be physical behaviors like hand washing or mental behaviors like rumination, is called a *compulsion* (American Psychiatric Association 2013). OCD can feel like a never-ending doom-and-gloom radio is on in your mind, one that loops your worst fears all day, every day, with no off button. It warns you of all the grave mistakes you could be making, have already made, or couldn't possibly stand to make—and if this sounds like torture, that's because it absolutely is. In fact, the World Health Organization once listed anxiety disorders, including OCD, as the sixth-largest contributor to nonfatal health loss globally (World Health Organization 2017).

OCD is excruciating, especially when left untreated, and it sounds something like this:

Brain:    What if you didn't mean it when you said "I love you" and you're actually just a liar and a fraud?

You:      Shoot. Good point, brain…did I really mean what I said? I thought I did, but now I'm not completely sure! That's bad, right? Shouldn't I know?

Brain:    Yes, very bad! We have a big problem here! If you don't figure this out, you'll end up loveless, alone, and miserable!

You:      Oh wow. Lovelessness is my worst fear! I have to know this answer, or else how can I continue in this relationship?

Brain:    That's right, you won't feel okay until you know. Better start digging!

And you're off! Ruminating, comparing, internet searching, doing anything you can to try to solve the questions of whether you really meant what you said and what it might mean if you're not 100 percent sure. Those nagging, doubting what-if thoughts you hear all day? The ones about the rightness of your partnership, the trueness of your feelings, or the way others seem to have it all figured out? Those are obsessions, and when they appear, they really do feel like a matter of life or death. Most people are familiar with OCD through its depiction in the media as compulsive cleanliness or organization, but the true scope of this disorder encompasses much more than just a desire to feel clean. In fact, the subject of intrusive thoughts in OCD can attach to just about anything, although it usually picks what you care about most. That's right! OCD doesn't just choose any message to send your way, a message that would be easy to ignore. Rather, it tends to fixate on our biggest fears and most terrifying outcomes, the ones that keep us up at night. It fixates on the sort of things that, if they were to occur, could lead to rejection, abandonment, or a lifetime of pain and suffering (or so OCD says).

Common OCD themes include the following:

**Relationship OCD (ROCD):** Fear of being in the wrong relationship, fear of not truly loving your partner, or fear of not being truly loved by your partner

**Sexual orientation OCD (SOOCD):** Fear of being the "wrong" sexual orientation or of being in denial about your true sexual orientation, previously known as homosexual OCD (HOCD)

**Harm OCD:** Fear of harming others, whether in the past or present, or fear of harming yourself or committing suicide

**Pedophile OCD (POCD):** Fear of sexually assaulting children, or fearing that you are secretly attracted to children and will act on it

**Existential OCD:** Fear of or preoccupation with the afterlife, the nature of existence, or other philosophical or existential inquiries

**Scrupulosity/hypermorality:** An excessive concern with being morally correct and good, often associated with religiosity or fear of eternal damnation

**Postpartum OCD**: Fear of intentionally or unintentionally hurting or even killing your child, a theme that often occurs for new mothers

**Health OCD**: Persistent fear that you could have a life-threatening illness, despite few or no symptoms—also known as hypochondria

Like an overprotective parent, OCD goes a few steps too far in its attempts to keep you safe, smothering you and paralyzing your ability to take risks. But before you look at this list and judge yourself too harshly, it's important to note that those with OCD do not choose to have it and that nothing you did in your life caused your heightened level of anxiety.

No matter how dark or disturbing the thoughts you have may be and no matter how uniquely flawed you may feel on your worst days, you are not a bad person simply for having intrusive thoughts. In fact, you couldn't be more fundamentally different from, for example, the kind of truly dangerous person who would violate, hurt, or intentionally harm others! That's because the intrusive thoughts in OCD (such as *What if I suffocate my baby?*) are considered *ego dystonic:* they go completely against the person's values, action, and true desires. It's unlikely, for example, that a murderous person would even be in therapy discussing their murderous thoughts, because they wouldn't register the thoughts as unwanted or intrusive, and they certainly would not receive an OCD diagnosis. Likewise, it's unlikely that a bad relationship filled with disrespect and toxicity would trigger ROCD. Having doubt in an unhealthy relationship is completely aligned, what we call *ego syntonic* thinking.

It's also worth noting that though we will dedicate this book to the exploration of a particular theme of OCD, there is no official diagnosis of relationship OCD in the fifth edition of the *Diagnostic and Statistical Manual (DSM-V)*, the official guidebook of diagnoses which mental health professionals turn to when assessing a case. That's because, fundamentally, all themes of obsessive-compulsive disorder—be they harm, sexual orientation, contamination, or relationship—are just different masks for the same condition. They are all part of the obsessive-compulsive spectrum, a cluster of symptoms that includes chronic doubt, heightened anxiety, and the use of compulsions to try to alleviate distress.

This shared parentage also explains why some people start out with one theme and then switch to another. For example, it's common to see a client who is currently struggling with ROCD also present with heightened distress around morality, worrying, for example, *Am I a horrible person for having these thoughts?* and then engaging in compulsive prayer to neutralize this fear. This same client might have experienced obsessions around sexual orientation, harm, symmetry, or any other theme at another point in their life. Themes can switch, show up in tandem, and even go away all on their own, and their lasting power usually depends on how much energy and attention we give them, how compulsively we behave when they arise in our mind. Think back to the last time an intrusive thought popped into your mind. Did you fight it? Did you try to solve it, or figure out the "right" answer? Or did you do the incredibly counterintuitive action of allowing that thought to exist, paying no attention to it whatsoever?

You might be able to guess which strategies get us in trouble, and the ones we'll aim to correct. And if obsessions are the hypothetical horror stories that pop into our mind unbidden, then all the things we do to clean up our intrusive thoughts, all the behaviors aimed at feeling better and finding an answer, are called compulsions. Being barraged with horror stories 24/7 will inevitably cause serious pain and discomfort, and it's instinctual to run and fight when we feel attacked. So it's only natural that you might spend hours googling what true love looks like or endlessly ask the people closest to you, "Do you think these thoughts are normal? Am I a horrible person for even thinking these things?"

Compulsive behaviors fall into four recognizable categories:

**Overt compulsions.** Obvious, external compulsions, the behaviors that people tend to recognize most noticeably as OCD. Overt compulsions are rituals or behaviors that are repeated many times until you achieve that *just-right* feeling. Common examples include:

| | |
|---|---|
| Hand washing | Compulsive organizing |
| Door checking | Tapping/touching |

**Avoidance compulsions.** Anytime you avoid anxiety by avoiding the trigger that would have caused it. Common examples include:

Avoiding intimacy for fear of having unwanted thoughts or not feeling "enough"

Avoiding committed statements toward your partner for fear of leading them on, when you are not 100 percent certain

Avoiding people you find attractive for fear of acting on an impulse

Avoiding romantic comedies or songs about love and instant attraction

**Reassurance-seeking compulsions.** Anytime you seek to reduce anxiety by seeking reassurance or an answer from others. Common examples include:

Excessive online searching of the problem or symptoms

Excessive discussion with others about your relationship

Confessing to having thoughts about the attractiveness of others or confessing to thoughts you worry are wrong or unfaithful

Checking and evaluating your physical reactions during sex for signs that you are having the right feelings toward your partner

**Mental compulsions/mental problem solving.** The most difficult of compulsions to identify and isolate, mental problem solving feels like overthinking. This kind of compulsion includes:

Mentally ruminating on the rightness of your relationship

Mentally trying to solve the problem of whether or not your partner is the right one for you; reviewing pros and cons

Mentally reviewing a situation to see if you acted or behaved in a way that would prove or disprove your love for your partner

Now that we've covered some of the most common obsessions and compulsions, take a moment to identify your own. Grab a notepad and see if you can think of what intrusive thoughts feel the most pressing right now and which compulsions you've been engaging in to try to alleviate the distress caused by those thoughts—all the ways you've been trying to wash your hands clean of doubt and discomfort. Do this before we go on, to explore exactly how compulsive behaviors like the ones listed earlier exacerbate your anxiety and keep you stuck in a worry loop.

**EXERCISE:** List the what-if obsessions you're currently experiencing on one side of a sheet of paper. Then, on the other side, list the corresponding compulsions you engage in to try to bring down the anxiety caused by those obsessions. Do you generally avoid, seek reassurance, or mentally ruminate when you feel triggered?

## How Compulsive Behavior Keeps Anxiety Alive

In the mid-twentieth century, researcher B.F. Skinner ran a series of studies to prove a learning process that came to be known as *operant conditioning,* a principle we use in almost every facet of life today. In these studies, Skinner placed lab rats in a small experimental cage (known as a Skinner box) that was outfitted with various features. For example, the Skinner box had a lever that would dispense food pellets when pushed, and it also had a button to turn on an electrified floor meant to deliver a small but uncomfortable shock to the rat as it moved about the cage. To start his experiment, Skinner introduced a hungry rat into the box and watched as it quickly made the connection that pushing the lever caused something good to happen (receiving a snack). He noticed that the rat learned to push the lever much faster than it would learn with no reinforcement at all or with a reinforcing agent of lower value, and the principle of *positive reinforcement* was discovered and named.

Then Skinner used his box to prove the other side of this same coin, a concept called *negative reinforcement*. He turned on the electrified floor and rewired the lever not to deliver tasty pellet snacks but to function as an off switch to stop the electric shock. Skinner measured both the time it took for the rat to get to the lever from the other side of the cage and the rat's desire to push the lever. As you can imagine, the rats were highly motivated to escape the discomfort of an electrified floor and quickly figured out that pushing the lever was the solution to end their pain. The rats pushed the lever—again and again and again. Sometimes they even ran to push the lever at the slightest hint that the electric floor might be turned on! These rats were not at all interested in tolerating discomfort.

Questionable ethics aside, Skinner proved a foundational principle of human learning, one you probably know at an intuitive level. He proved that any behavior followed by a pleasant consequence is likely to be repeated and that the avoidance of pain is a powerful motivator for rat (and human) behavior. This principle also explains why we engage in compulsions. Like the rats in Skinner's experiment, we experience relief (pellets) when we engage in a compulsion that temporarily eases our anxiety and are much more likely to engage in that same compulsion the next time around. We've also learned that one way to stop the electrified floor of our intrusive thoughts and feelings is to avoid, to ruminate, or to seek reassurance—to push any lever that we can to escape our discomfort.

Of course, human behavior is far more complex than rat behavior, and what motivates each person to engage in compulsions is unique. But at the core, the same principle of reinforcement and pain avoidance applies to all of us. Unlike our lab friends, however, we are capable of recognizing and rising above our instincts—we can play the long game, the one that ultimately leads to a far greater reward than a few momentary pellets, the one that sets us free.

Figure 1 shows the reinforcing pattern of OCD:

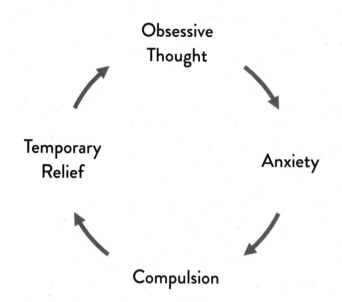

**Figure 1:** Obsessive-Compulsive Cycle

Let's imagine you have an intrusive thought, something like *My partner botches words in conversation with our friends and doesn't catch literary references. What if she's not at my intellectual level, and I'll always find our connection lacking?* Or, more simply, *We're not compatible.* Naturally, this intrusive thought produces a lot of anxiety for you as someone who loves their partner and desperately wants to feel good about the choice they've made. Maybe you think you shouldn't be having these thoughts, or believe that true love requires perfect compatibility. Whatever the reason, you're anxious, and your first instinct is to do something about that anxiety, to escape the negative stimulus hammering your nervous system.

So you proceed to subtly quiz your partner on vocabulary words and philosophical concepts over dinner that night. The quizzing is a form of reassurance seeking that at first doesn't seem to be too harmful. In fact, maybe quizzing your partner provides temporary relief as she answers most of your sneaky questions correctly, proving she's not as uninformed as your anxiety had feared! You feel good, relieved even, and for the next hour or for the rest of the night your anxiety is blissfully quiet. *That* solved it! Or so you think—because deep in your neural wiring, your brain is beginning to make a very unhelpful connection. It's beginning to think that anxiety can be solved—we just have to do whatever it takes to get there! We just have to push the lever a few hundred more times. And so, the next time that same anxious thought arises, you repeat the same compulsion. Except maybe this time the nagging question *Are you sure they're smart enough?* comes back around sooner, after fifteen minutes instead of twenty, and is accompanied by a new worry, something like *You're making an awful lot of excuses. Are you sure you should even be thinking something like that about someone you claim to love?* Right back into compulsions you go! Stuck in an ever-tightening loop.

Yes, compulsions temporarily grant relief, but they cause big problems in the long term. Because when we engage in any kind of compulsive behavior, we reinforce two very dangerous messages in our brain:

1. By acting on an intrusive thought, we validate and legitimize it. Your brain thinks, *She responded when I sent out that what-if thought, so it must be something important and meaningful. I'll keep sending it!*

2. By refusing to tolerate the anxiety triggered by the intrusive thought or feeling, we reinforce our inability to cope with pain. We reinforce a false belief that we can't handle the possible feared outcome, that we're not strong enough to cope.

The more we validate our brain's fearful thinking and invalidate our ability to cope with it, the bigger our anxiety grows, the more powerful and consuming it becomes. The more powerful the anxiety becomes, the harder it is to tolerate and the more likely we are to try and escape it through compulsion. This cycle continues viciously onward, and we become stuck, like a parent who keeps giving their crying child candy to quiet them, only to see the behavior grow out of control.

Houston! We've got a problem. But we also have a solution. Part 2 of this book will give you the exact tools and strategies needed to help you tolerate discomfort and stop reinforcing anxious messaging. First, we need to review a few ground rules:

1.  You can't control thoughts.

2.  You can never control the feelings that accompany these thoughts.

3.  You can control one thing and one thing only, and that is your reaction to thoughts and feelings.

Thankfully, this is enough. And when you stop reinforcing the absolute need for certainty at the heart of anxiety, your OCD will begin to die down. When you cut compulsions, you teach your brain that the messages it sends you about the rightness of your relationship or the trueness of your love just aren't that important! The thing is that while healing anxiety is simple in theory, it can be quite complicated in practice. That's because, along the way, you'll inevitably come up against the incredible power of your own instincts, force of habit, and, of course, the biggest block to freedom—the fear of making a mistake. More so, you can count on anxiety to be there at every single turn in your recovery, whispering, imploring, and then screaming at you to listen. *Danger! You're making the biggest mistake of your life!* You'll have to hear it all and walk forward anyway.

## ROCD and the Soul Mate

Treating all themes of OCD takes this same amount of incredible courage, so why write an entire book specifically for ROCD? Because in more than a decade of specializing in the treatment of anxiety disorders, I've found that successfully treating ROCD requires more than just the elimination of compulsive behaviors. The most powerful approach to the treatment of relationship anxiety and ROCD asks that we redefine what we expect and require from our relationships, that we bring not only our anxiety back to scale, but also our expectations of what love and partnership should provide. We live in a time when romantic love and the pursuit of a soul mate have taken on an almost spiritual importance, and we rely on infatuation to elevate us above the relative normalcy of daily human life. It's no longer sufficient to have a good-enough life or a good-enough love story. We want the Hollywood version and won't settle for anything less. As the Jungian philosopher Robert Johnson puts it, "Romantic love is the single greatest energy system in the Western psyche. In our culture it has supplanted religion as the arena in which men and women seek meaning, transcendence, wholeness, and ecstasy" (1983, xi).

That's a lot of pressure to place on another person, isn't it? Be my lover, friend, savior, emotional support, intellectual equal: *be it all.* It's so much pressure, in fact, that the most effective approach to understanding and treating ROCD must take this incredibly strong cultural programming—the Myth of the One—into consideration if we hope to heal. By upending our expectations of what partnership should be, we release the pressure valve and give anxiety much less reason to sound the alarm. In the next chapter, we'll explore the roots of MOTO and the ways in which ROCD is colored by this fascination with romantic love. We'll aim to understand why ROCD is showing up now, in this particular relationship, and also take a stab at one of the most pressing concerns in relationship anxiety: *How do I know this is really anxiety and that I'm not just in denial?*

Before we dive more fully into relationship OCD, take a moment to complete the Relationship Obsessive-Compulsive Inventory (ROCI) (Doron, et al. 2012). This test is not meant to act as a substitute for proper assessment, only a qualified mental health professional can provide an official diagnosis. Rather, use it to confirm what you might already know. Higher numbers are an indicator that your constant doubts could be more than just cold feet.

## ROCI—RELATIONSHIP OBSESSIVE-COMPULSIVE INVENTORY

Rate the degree to which each statement reflects your own experience, on a scale of 0 to 4:

| Not at all | A little | Moderately | A lot | Very much |
|:---:|:---:|:---:|:---:|:---:|
| 0 | 1 | 2 | 3 | 4 |

| | | |
|:---:|:---|:---:|
| 1. | The thought that I don't really love my partner haunts me. | |
| 2. | I find it easy to dismiss my doubts about my partner. | |
| 3. | I constantly doubt my relationship. | |
| 4. | I find it difficult to dismiss doubts regarding my partner's love for me. | |
| 5. | I check and recheck whether my relationship feels "right." | |
| 6. | I am constantly looking for evidence that my partner really loves me. | |
| 7. | I feel that I must remind myself over and over again why I love my partner. | |
| 8. | I am sure my partner loves me. | |
| 9. | I am extremely disturbed by thoughts that something is "not right" in my relationship. | |
| 10. | I continuously doubt my love for my partner. | |
| 11. | I keep asking my partner whether they really love me. | |
| 12. | I frequently seek reassurance that my relationship is "right." | |
| 13. | I am constantly bothered by the thought that my partner doesn't really want to be with me. | |
| 14. | I feel a need to repeatedly check how much I love my partner. | |

# CHAPTER 2

# Relationship Anxiety

Relationships matter. Good ones inspire us, creating a safe emotional space where we can grow and explore ourselves and the world around us. Being in a loving partnership is correlated with health, well-being, and even longevity (Stavrova 2019). Bad relationships, on the other hand, can traumatize us, limit our potential, and destroy our sense of self. But in our modern world, finding and maintaining the right relationship has become more than just a worthwhile goal; it's become a full-time preoccupation. It's clear that, for better or for worse, the quality of our relationships matters more to us now than at any other time in the human story. And while there are plenty of reasons to celebrate the shift we've made from viewing partnership as merely a way to secure wealth and status, what if we've found ourselves at the other end of the spectrum? I can't help but notice these days that finding and maintaining the right relationship doesn't just matter; it matters too much. So much that it's triggering massive amounts of anxiety and fueling a crisis of relational dissatisfaction.

Take a look around, and it's easy to see why. Through the movies, music, and media we consume, through the expectations of those around us, and through the very culture itself, we receive an almost constant stream of messaging about the ecstasy of infatuation and its ability to save us and make us whole. We are exposed to the magical properties of romantic love in so many implicit and explicit ways that expecting MOTO levels of perfection in a relationship seems the absolute norm, not the exception. Of course, there's nothing wrong with a good love story, and there are real-life examples of partnership that fit the Hollywood narrative. But the truth for most of us is that the myth of perfect love and the need to achieve it are counterproductive to relational health and satisfaction. Holding our relationships to the MOTO standard typically makes us *less* satisfied in love, not more. And while it may feel like butterflies and soul mates have always been a part of the human story, would it surprise you to learn that this particular standard, what we'll call romantic love, is a relatively new one?

## A Modern History of Love

Romantic love was not always the cultural obsession that it is today. In fact, until the mid-nineteenth century, the flush of infatuation, the googly eyes, and "always and forever" were mostly looked upon as flights of fancy and relegated to the role of mistresses and extramarital affairs. For the vast majority of humanity, partnership was an economic endeavor meant to ensure the survival of two families and was entirely decided upon not by the young people themselves, but by parents looking out for their family's survival. Falling in love with your partner was a plus, but it was certainly not the primary goal of marriage. Your job was to marry at or above your social status, have a family, and till the fields until the day that you died, which was usually somewhere between thirty-five and fifty, depending upon how wealthy you were and how much access to food and healthcare you could afford.

Our ancestors simply didn't have the luxury of romantic love as we know it today, and it wasn't until the Industrial Revolution in the late eighteenth century that things began to shift. Up until then, almost 80 percent of the population of any given economy was employed in agrarian tasks like farming, food production, and livestock management. But by 1860, this number had plummeted to only about 20 percent, representing a massive shift in the way most people lived their lives. In their new city lives, young people were no longer tied to the land or dependent on villages for survival and could make their wealth (and their decisions) independent of their families. Collectivistic goals (what is good for the entire family) began to cede power to personal goals (what is good for the individual), and this is when romantic love began to shift from an enjoyable daydream into the primary purpose of partnership. Of course, tales of love, romance, and passion in literature date many centuries back and span many cultures, but these stories were fantasy to those who read them and in no way indicative of what most individuals expected out of their long-term relationships. With the luxury of financial and physical independence and the loss of the village, people began to expect more than just partnership: they began to expect it all.

As life moved from country to city, and from the demands of the day-to-day to the daydream, we began to place even more importance on finding deep fulfillment in our romantic relationships. We began to ask of one person what our entire village would have provided, all the various roles of friend, lover, partner, and coparent rolled into one special person whom we've come to call The One. Renowned couples therapist and speaker Esther Perel described this shift in a 2013 TED Talk: "We basically are asking [our partners] to give us what once an entire village used to provide: Give me belonging, give me identity, give me continuity, but give me transcendence and mystery and awe all in one. Give me comfort, give me edge. Give me novelty, give me familiarity. Give me predictability, give me surprise. And we think it's a given, and toys and lingerie are going to save us."

In the twentieth century, media and advertisers caught on to the power of the passion narrative to sell everything from films to perfume to cars, and MOTO became big business. A picture-perfect love story was not only a beautiful fantasy, but also now a narrative that made some people incredibly rich. Don Draper, the 1950s advertising agent from the TV series *Mad Men*, captures the essence of this shift when he tells a hopeful young woman, "What you call love was invented by guys like me to sell nylons." By the mid-twentieth century, what might have been disregarded as a flight of fancy just a hundred years earlier had become the standard of true love in the westernized world. And since we were assured this perfect person did, in fact, exist (thanks, Don), partnering with anyone who didn't meet the standard became a sure sign you had settled for less than you deserve, that you had settled for less than true love.

Of course, this seismic shift in our definition of partnership was and continues to be positive in many ways. For many young people, it meant a ticket out of a loveless, duty-filled existence. It represented a shift toward the power and importance of the individual and was a joyful assertion that life could be more than just survival, that we could hope for more. But somewhere along the way, the prospect of a more fulfilling, egalitarian, and passionate partnership evolved past preference and became a mandate. Today, it has become the only worthwhile way to be in partnership. And while the importance of finding the right relationship affects everyone, in the anxious mind, it morphs into something much more. It morphs into a question that must be solved and a burning need to know, which blots out your ability to see your relationship clearly, so consumed are you with measuring up. Relationship anxiety, that exaggerated need to get it right, clouds your ability to hold the duality of the complex person you've partnered with: the good with the bad, the practical with the passionate. Somewhere along the way, we went a bit too far.

It's important to note that our fascination with romantic love and its curative properties is primarily a Western preoccupation, though our influence is spreading fast. Partnership in the non-westernized world continues to be influenced by collectivistic goals and includes a heavy emphasis on familial match, socioeconomic compatibility, and comparable educational backgrounds. Interestingly, while we tend to judge these so-called arranged marriages (today, the family has a say but doesn't necessarily make the final call) as forced and loveless, studies have shown that they are equal to free-choice marriages (in which a person finds and chooses their partner on their own) in levels of satisfaction, overall happiness, and affection (Regan, Lakhanpal, and Anguiano 2012). Perhaps this is because, while infatuation is unarguably exciting and thrilling, the best matches, the ones that work in the long term, reflect qualities that might seem more mundane at first glance: qualities like a partner's psychological flexibility, long-term compatibility, and willingness to tolerate and work through times of difficulty and stress.

You know, the sort of qualities that don't make for a good movie or a catchy love song.

## The Trouble with Butterflies

Before you write me off as heartless, let me be clear. I *love* love. I cheer at weddings, tear up watching romantic comedies, and have a deep and enduring passion for *Titanic*-era Leonardo DiCaprio. But I also know that there's more to loving someone than MOTO would have us believe. There's more to good relationships than infatuation and butterflies, feelings that might or might not have been there in your relationship, feelings that are all but guaranteed to be ephemeral (Tennov 1979). That's because that butterfly feeling, the exhilarating emptiness in your gut that has become the cornerstone of our MOTO fantasies, has absolutely no correlation with long-term happiness, sexual satisfaction, or compatibility in a relationship. No doubt, your butterflies are indicators of excitement and nervousness, and, yes, those are rousing emotions to feel at the start of a relationship. It's just that neither excitement nor nervousness is a true indicator of what that person will ultimately mean to you and how well the two of you might navigate life as a team.

Interestingly, the magical feeling of butterflies comes from the very same part of our brain responsible for registering threat and fear—the very same portion responsible for our anxiety—the amygdala. That's right! Feelings of anticipation and threat in the amygdala translate to the knotting sensation in the stomach that we've come to call butterflies. We experience butterflies when jumping out of a plane, giving an important presentation, or preparing for an interview. They are not a rare occurrence, but when we feel them in the context of romance, we've been taught to view the feeling as a marker of importance, as a sign that we have potentially found The One. But here's the thing: *not* feeling that particular butterfly brand of anxiety when meeting a potential life partner isn't always a bad sign. In fact, for many, it could be exactly what the doctor ordered.

Imagine if you grew up walking on eggshells, always watching what you said or did, and finally met someone who was not a perpetuation of that cycle of instability, someone who instead felt like a safe and secure place. If this person didn't inspire nervousness and excitement, it's likely others around you would say, "You just don't seem that into it." And you, too, might worry about the lack of fireworks, not because those feelings are accurate harbingers of happiness but because you've come to see them as such. So what happens when you meet exactly this sort of person, the sort of person with all the right ingredients to become a life partner, the sort of person you'd really like to be with but who doesn't trigger those MOTO feelings—the ones we've been taught are the ultimate indicators of true love? What happens when the anxiety you feel toward them seems disproportionally large, making it all but impossible to stay connected and relax into vulnerability and, thus, into love?

What happens, of course, is ROCD, a theme of obsessive compulsive disorder that fixates on the rightness of your partnership and the trueness of your love for your partner or of their love for you.

## Understanding ROCD

ROCD can keep you from having the sort of connection, intimacy, and love you deserve—not the MOTO kind but something richer—a real-life love story filled with challenges, imperfections, and profound personal growth. ROCD, like all forms of OCD, involves the presence of obsessions and compulsions, and can feel like an overwhelming urge to solve or answer the burning question *How do I know if I'm truly in the right relationship?* This preoccupation with perfect love can be seen as two interrelated subtypes.

## Partner-Focused and Relationship-Focused ROCD

In *partner-focused* ROCD, the primary preoccupation is with your partner's perceived flaws, while *relationship-focused* ROCD fixates on the overall quality or temperature of the relationship (Doron, Derby, and Szepsenwol 2014).

Here are some common partner-focused obsessions:

- *My partner looks less attractive to me right now. Maybe we don't have sexual chemistry and would be better off as friends?*

- *My partner isn't as ambitious or motivated as other men I've dated. Should I look for someone more career oriented?*

- *She isn't my type. I'm usually into tall brunettes. Maybe that's why I'm not feeling certain about our relationship?*

- *They are quiet and reserved around my friends. What if everyone thinks my partner is boring and that I've settled for less than I deserve?*

Here are common obsessions in relationship-focused ROCD:

- *I don't have butterflies when I look at my partner. Does this mean something is wrong with my relationship?*

- *My partner isn't paying the same amount of attention to me that they once were. Does this mean they are losing interest and our relationship is doomed?*

- *I can't get fully aroused when we are intimate. Does this mean we are not sexually compatible?*

- *That couple we know seems so happy, they must have that in-love feeling and just know they are right for one another. Why don't I feel this in my relationship?*

- *I don't find myself missing my partner as much as I did my ex. This must be proof I'm just not that into it.*

The examples given here are just a small sample of the thousands of different obsessions one can experience with ROCD, and there's plenty of overlap between partner-focused and relationship-focused obsessions. In fact, these two subtypes often inform and exacerbate one another, which is why we rarely delineate between them in treatment, and in this book I'll refer to them more generally as ROCD. It's also important to note that while this book is dedicated to romantic relationships, which represent the overwhelming majority of ROCD cases, it is possible to have relational obsessions about the degree of love you feel toward a child, a friend, or even a pet.

## Common Reactions

It's clear that, regardless of what subtype your obsessions may fall into, these thoughts are all incredibly distressing. They are not the sort of thoughts you would ever want to be having toward someone you care about, and experiencing them may leave you anxious, confused, and desperate for relief. And even though you now understand that compulsions aren't helpful, during an anxiety spike, they may still feel like the only solution.

Common compulsions in ROCD include:

- Checking to see if you are in love enough with your partner

- Checking and comparing your relationship to others or to your past relationships

- Seeking reassurance from friends and family members about the rightness of your partnership

- Searching online to find signs that your partner may or may not be The One

- Ruminating on the rightness of your feelings or the temperature of the relationship

- Avoiding sex or intimacy for fear of getting triggered

- Avoiding committed statements or actions

- Repeatedly asking your partner if they love you

- Avoiding spending time with attractive people for fear that you will find them more appealing than your partner

Remember that these compulsions *will* bring you temporary relief. They will work in the short term. But that short-term relief only serves to increase the damaging message of OCD: that you really need perfect certainty to have a meaningful relationship and that you just are not capable of handling the discomfort of the unknown. As with all forms of anxiety and OCD treatment, these compulsions have got to go; later on in this book, you'll learn exactly how to challenge and ultimately eradicate them. And while it may be tempting to look at these thoughts and behaviors and feel like the worst person in the world, to feel crazy or messed up, remember that to do so ignores a fundamental truth: you have absolutely no control over the content of what your brain throws at you or over the painful feelings that result. You didn't want or ask for this experience, and these thoughts are not necessarily indicators of what you truly think and how you truly feel.

Nope! The intrusive thoughts and compulsive behaviors seen in ROCD don't make you a bad partner or a horrible person. Quite the contrary, having these thoughts in the context of a relationship is incredibly normal, so much so that every single person you know has experienced such doubts at times in their relationship. Everyone has worried about compatibility or attraction, about whether their relationship measures up or if they could be happier with someone else. That's because these are human concerns, generally unspoken but nonetheless perfectly normal. The difference is that, in the OCD brain, these thoughts feel stickier. They feel more urgent and important, and the consequence of *not* figuring them out feels more dire. Anxiety has a sneaky way of getting our attention: it will exaggerate the possibility of threat (*You've got to figure this out now, or else!*) while simultaneously minimizing our belief in our ability to cope with it (*You can't possibly tolerate the unknown. It's just too scary!*).

Quite the one-two punch, isn't it?

We can thank our amygdala, the fear center of the human brain, for that little number. Remember, in chapter 1, we explored the biological and genetic origins of a hyperactive amygdala: how this portion of our brain meant to keep us safe and warn us of potential threat can be a bit smothering at times, like an overprotective parent nagging you to take a sweater "or you'll freeze to death!" But there's a second half to the story of why some people can enter into relationships free of anxiety, intrusive thoughts, and gut-wrenching anxiety, while others are left to wonder endlessly what's wrong with their partner or, worse, what's wrong with them. Our childhood environments have a massive impact on the relationship anxiety we feel as adults, and understanding this piece of the puzzle can be key to healing from it.

## How Upbringing Influences ROCD

Before diving into all things nurture, it's important to recognize that not everyone will relate to this piece of the puzzle. You may feel that you had a perfectly good childhood, with loving and available parents. Remember that anxiety is biological as well as environmental, and there's not always an outside trigger we can identify as the culprit. If you grew up in a peaceful and loving home, you might feel relationship anxiety for the simple reason that relationships are deeply important to you and greatly impact your quality of life, and your anxious brain knows it. Relationships are inherently risky, and good ones demand a level of vulnerability rarely required anywhere else in our lives. Good relationships ask us to trust and take leap of faith after leap of faith into the wild unknown, never certain we'll land in one piece. And that risk is often the only fuel our brains need to begin warning us of potential downsides and possible red flags—no backstory necessary!

However, for most of the clients I work with, the ROCD they feel is a combination of nature and nurture, with roots tracing back to their earliest days in this world, back to the days when they, like all of us, were dependent on their caregivers for every aspect of survival. As humans, we enter this world practically helpless, unable to lift our heads for the first four months of life or to sit unaided until about nine months after birth. In contrast, baby giraffes can run from a predator the very day they are born! This extreme vulnerability requires an equally extreme survival mechanism, and so humans evolved to stay in connection to their caregivers at all times. We evolved a complex psychological attachment system aimed at getting our every need met from the most important people in the universe, our caregivers. This adaptation toward extreme attachment means that, as humans, we are especially vulnerable to the influence of our caregivers.

In many ways, our childhood experiences become the blueprint (though not the mandate) for our adult perspective and our adult relationships, which is why any therapist you visit will ask you about your childhood and how you were parented. Your upbringing matters a lot in the formation of the person you are today; it informs why you do what you do and how you see the world. It also informs your fears and anxieties and the blocks and defenses you might have developed to get through your childhood, all while staying in connection to caregivers, while maintaining attachment. In fact, studies on ROCD have shown a significant correlation between attachment injuries, or traumas, that occurred in these primary relationships and higher levels of relationship anxiety and distress (Doron, et al. 2012).

The groundbreaking theory of attachment, originated in 1958 by John Bowlby and later expanded upon by Mary Ainsworth, describes the way in which our early connection (or lack thereof) to our caregivers manifests in four distinct attachment styles (Ainsworth 1978):

**Secure attachment:** One or both caregivers were generally present and available, allowing their child space to explore the world around them and safely make mistakes while also being available to soothe them and provide protection if something scary happened during that exploration. Securely attached adults tend to have healthy adult relationships. They identify with the following statements taken from the Experiences in Close Relationships scale (Fraley et al. 2011):

- *I feel comfortable sharing my private thoughts and feelings with my partner.*

- *I rarely worry about my partner leaving me.*

- *I am very comfortable being close to romantic partners.*

- *It helps to turn to my romantic partner in times of need.*

**Anxious attachment:** One or both caregivers were generally unavailable or neglectful, either emotionally or physically, leaving their child to crave connection and experience a sense of rejection or unlovability. Anxiously attached adults are often the pursuer in relationships and often worry that they're not worthy or deserving of love. They identify with these statements (Fraley et al. 2011):

- *I'm afraid that I will lose my partner's love.*

- *I often worry that my partner will not want to stay with me.*

- *I often worry that my partner doesn't really love me.*

- *I worry that romantic partners won't care about me as much as I care about them.*

**Avoidant attachment:** One or both caregivers were generally overwhelming or overbearing in their parenting style and might have overstepped boundaries to have their own need for love served by the relationship with their child. As adults, the children of these caregivers can find connection overwhelming, and they worry that they might lose their autonomy. They often identify as the distancer in a relational dynamic and can be aloof and highly independent. They relate to these statements (Fraley et al. 2011):

- *I prefer not to show a partner how I feel deep down.*

- *I find it difficult to allow myself to depend on romantic partners.*

- *I don't feel comfortable opening up to romantic partners.*

- *I prefer not to be too close to romantic partners.*

**Disorganized attachment**: One or both caregivers were abusive, inconsistent, or chaotic in their parenting style. This caregiver might have suffered from a personality disorder or struggled with addiction and may have been loving one day but neglectful or even cruel the next. As adults, the children of these caregivers crave connection but also fear it; they identify with statements from both the anxious and the avoidant styles, finding both intimacy and distance highly distressing.

## Finding a Way Forward

Wouldn't it be wonderful if we all came from households where our caregivers were able to attune to our emotional needs the vast majority of the time—if we were all raised in environments in which our needs were consistently met? Of course it would. But while a secure attachment style describes about 50 percent of the human population, for the other half, this just isn't the case (Hazan and Shaver 1994). This is the half that may find adult relationships particularly tricky, the half that is prone to relationship anxiety and ROCD. When you pair an insecure attachment style (avoidant, anxious, or disorganized) with a genetically hyperactive amygdala, the stakes can feel incredibly high in your relationship. ROCD is exactly what happens when you mix attachment anxiety with a natural predisposition to fear. It is a complex knot of nature, nurture, culture, and MOTO programming, and while it can all sound a bit dizzying to untangle, there is absolutely a way forward.

Although it may be hard to see the light at the end of the tunnel just yet, neither an insecure attachment style nor a hyperactive amygdala means you are doomed to a life of lovelessness or pain. In fact, Bowlby and Ainsworth in their work discovered that it is possible to gain *earned security* by partnering with someone who heals your unmet needs, someone who can provide the safety and security you didn't get growing up (Ainsworth 1978). That's right! You can literally change your attachment style and untangle childhood trauma by partnering with a healthy and consistent person. Remember that partner we talked about earlier? The one who wasn't scary and didn't trigger the butterflies? The one who felt instead like a safe and secure place to rest? That's the one. And while I'm not saying that finding a healthy person with a secure base means your relationship will be easy and free of anxiety, I am saying that this is exactly the sort of partner with whom you can heal. This is exactly the sort of partnership that can show you that your connection doesn't need to hurt and that stable, secure love is absolutely possible.

So what are the qualities you should be looking for? What sort of relationships have a deep security and health that can heal your relationship anxiety, as long as you're willing to put in the work?

**EXERCISE:** Here are some questions I ask my ROCD clients when they first come to treatment, questions that I use to determine whether or not a relationship has a healthy base. As you read, take a moment to think about your relationship (or a past relationship, if you're not currently in one) and what response you would give to the following questions:

- Are you in a loving, caring relationship where you are treated with respect and kindness?

- Does your partner seem to care about and try to understand your needs? Do they show a willingness to work on themselves when and if they miss the mark?

- Are you confused by the doubts and negative thoughts running through your mind, given the fundamental connection you feel with your partner?

- Is your partnership one in which the two members generally have shared interests and a shared vision for the future?

- Are you experiencing thoughts about your relationship that you find intrusive or unwanted and are fundamentally against the core warm feelings you experience in your partnership?

- Does the level of anxiety you are experiencing feel out of line with the level of real or perceived danger that dating your partner actually presents?

If you, like my clients, answered yes to most of these questions, it's likely that your relationship has a healthy base.

A healthy base alone is not enough to make a relationship work, and simply partnering with someone who is secure will not heal your insecure attachment style. But the relational qualities listed in this exercise are an important starting point.

Of course, your relationship anxiety will be standing in the way, telling you that the risk isn't worth taking and that the only way to feel safe in a relationship is to find the perfect person, the one who won't trigger any anxiety in the first place. But given that you've picked up this book, it seems likely that, at some point in time, you will need to untangle this psychological knot. At some point, whether now or ten years in the future, you will realize that ROCD makes an appearance whenever the risk of vulnerability and love exist; it shows up in your healthy romantic relationships. Eventually, you may come to see that your anxiety says much less about the person you are with than it does about your relationship to vulnerability itself.

## Why ROCD Is Happening Now

One of the more perplexing parts of experiencing relationship doubts and obsessions is that they might not have always been present in your previous relationships. Think of how confusing treating ROCD becomes when some of our relationships feel completely free and easy while others are riddled with fear! If you've ever wondered why ROCD decides to show up in some relationships but not others, you may identify with my client Claire.

> *Claire, an actress in her late twenties, came to treatment shortly after she started dating Kamal. She described Kamal as cute, funny, and quirky—the kind of person she could see a future with and with whom she enjoyed spending time as long as her anxiety wasn't in the way. In her intake session, Claire reported having OCD symptoms since she was young, mostly around contamination and organization. She also described being raised in a home where making the exact right move was expected at all times, a home where mistakes were reacted to poorly. And while Claire didn't have much anxiety at the beginning of her relationship with Kamal, as the intensity and commitment escalated, she reported feeling more distressed, withdrawn, and irritable. She began to find the tone of Kamal's voice annoying and noticed his style of dress and hair wasn't quite up-to-date. Claire constantly commented on Kamal's appearance, touching and fixing his hair, especially when they would go out in public, and she noticed that she was tense whenever Kamal didn't look or dress exactly the way she liked. Claire worried this was all a sign that she was not truly in love. "I didn't have these thoughts and feelings with my exes," she said. "If this is really OCD, then why didn't it show up earlier?"*

It was easy for me to see why Claire could feel fearful in her new relationship. With Kamal, there was a real possibility she could be hurt—not because he was a bad guy, but quite the opposite—because he was an available, compatible, and loving partner. Kamal was actually someone Claire could see herself falling in love with! And though it might not have appeared this way on the outside, her previous relationships were actually quite safe by comparison. That's because, deep down, Claire knew that her past partners were not ready, not willing, or not able to join her in the risk of love, and thus she could freely access her positive emotions toward them. For example, she had briefly dated a man who was significantly older than she was and didn't want any more children (Claire always wanted her own kids), while another partner was nowhere near ready to settle down. In these relationships, Claire frequently took on the pursuer role—running toward someone who didn't reciprocate the intensity of her feelings. Because these people were emotionally unavailable, she had the space to feel love, attraction, and desire. She felt free to love without the fear that she would actually be asked to face and overcome her fear of vulnerability. There was no need for ROCD to ever make an appearance!

Your ROCD has shown up now precisely because you are in something (or about to start something) that might actually have sea legs. You are with the sort of person and partner you could actually love, someone who activates your attachment insecurities because this person is worth letting your guard down for. Remember that your anxiety, irrational as it may seem at times, is trying its best to keep you safe. It is an alarm that turns on at the possibility of pain, which is why it's the healthy, available relationships that activate your amygdala and produce that painful barrage of intrusive thoughts and feelings asking *But are you sure?* Anxiety would prefer you to stay comfortable, in safe but ultimately fruitless relationships. It would rather not face the pain, rejection, and unmet needs of childhood, and it certainly would prefer if you didn't attempt to grow and evolve, thank you very much! All relationships carry risk, but if you're experiencing ROCD now, it could be because you have found the sort of relationship that is scary for all the *right* reasons. You may have found a risk worth taking.

This is exactly why good ROCD treatment asks that we stop reinforcing the importance of finding The One and perfecting our partner and that we get comfortable with the itchy, scratchy gray area instead. It asks that we risk trusting that our anxiety around relationships is not about whether our partner is smart enough, attractive enough, interesting enough, or compatible enough, but about whether they expose our psychological wounds. And though it might not sound like a MOTO love story, the gray area is where true love flourishes. It's where we accept uncertainty, imperfection, and discomfort and choose to head into the unknown with the person we have chosen, come what may.

Kind of romantic, eh?

So why don't we just make the switch? If we know our expectations of love aren't realistic, and our pursuit of perfection is just a defense mechanism meant to shield us from possible pain and rejection, why don't we abandon our fears and jump headlong into healthier partnership? For one thing, changing this wiring is hard. It's counterintuitive to walk toward fear and ignore the powerful signals of distress that anxiety sends our way; we're simply not wired to do so. It requires hundreds of leaps into the unknown to take an intellectual belief that you'll be safe and turn that into intuitive knowing, into a felt sense of trust that you can, indeed, tolerate the gray area, no matter what anxiety says. It takes work to realize that no matter what happens in your relationship, no matter what you feel or don't at the end of the day, no matter if you stay together for life or separate after a few years, you are capable and able to cope with the outcome of your decisions. And it takes wisdom to recognize that the greatest risk of all may not be in choosing and committing to that process of discovery, but in the life lost while looking for the perfect next step.

If you still balk at the idea of doing this work, it might be because, deep down, you are not yet 100 percent convinced what you're feeling is truly ROCD at all. You might not be sure. And even if you've identified with everything you've read thus far, my guess is that there's probably a nagging voice in the back of your head throwing more doubt your way, doubting this whole process! Maybe it says something to the effect of *This isn't really ROCD. That's just a lie you're making up. It's pretty clear that you don't really love your partner and you're just in denial. If you listen to this lady and start ignoring me, you'll also be ignoring the truth.*

Yikes. No one wants to dupe themselves into loving someone and wake up a decade later with two kids and a mortgage, only to realize they've made the biggest mistake of their lives. No one wants to fool an innocent and perfectly nice bystander into a life of lovelessness and deceit. And despite how accurately your symptoms line up with the diagnostic criteria for ROCD, you'd probably like to be sure that you're not ignoring an important internal message. You'd like to be sure that, by following the strategies in this book, you're not just numbing yourself to the truth because you're too scared to face it or you're too insecure to go after someone you really want to be with, the perfect person. How then can you be sure that, by healing your ROCD, you're not shutting out a warning signal meant to stop you from making the biggest mistake of your life?

You can't be sure, and there just isn't a perfect answer to this very anxiety-producing question. No relationship specialist, anxiety expert, pastor, psychic, or prophet can decide for you if you've chosen correctly. No one can guarantee that the partner you've chosen will satisfy you for the rest of your life or always meet your needs (in fact, I can more confidently promise that they won't and that you'll have to work through it together). And no one can guarantee that what you're experiencing is high anxiety and not just a fancy form of denial. But here's the thing: if you are in a fundamentally healthy partnership, one that meets most but not all of your needs, one that offers respect, support, appreciation, love, and a shared vision for the future, you might not need the answer to that question. You might not need to know if you've really found The One. You might be able to see that, with most (but not all!) of the right ingredients, what comes next is up to you, and that there is no such thing as the right partner, but only the relationship and person you choose to see as such.

Will you ever feel certainty about your relationship? Maybe, if you don't go looking for it. But the reality is that for most people in recovery from ROCD, the answer to that question becomes irrelevant. They stop searching and endlessly checking if they've made the right decision and begin to enjoy their partner exactly the way they are, imperfections and all. And if doing the work in this book gives you the connection, intimacy, and love you've always wanted, would you still need to know with absolute certainty if you had made the right match? Could you tolerate the gray area if it meant you would finally be at peace? Because at the end of the day, it's up to you and your partner to heal old wounds together and to turn compatibility, chemistry, connection, and mutual respect into a love story for the ages. It's up to you to cultivate, rather than find, the ideal partner. The good news is that doing so is entirely possible.

It just might not look exactly the way you thought it would.

# CHAPTER 3

# Sex Anxiety

My guess is that when you chose your partner and dreamed of a future together, you didn't intend on having a threesome (at least not right away), and yet, despite your best attempts to kick it out, there anxiety sits at the end of your bed, a very unwelcome third wheel. Maybe it whispers insecurities in your ear as you touch one another, or it slides in between you and your partner and reminds you of all the things you're *not* feeling and of all the past experiences you might have had with other people, endlessly checking to see if the experience you're having is the right experience, with all the right feelings. Anxiety makes sure to pipe in just as you begin to loosen up and asks, *Was the way your ex did this more enjoyable?* It wonders, infuriatingly, *Shouldn't you be more into this?*

Anxiety is all too skilled at pulling you out of your bodily experience and right back up where it wants you, in your head and caught up in thoughts. If you have ROCD, it's likely that you experience intrusive thinking during sex and about sex at other times, a false alarm that goes off when you imagine getting intimate with the person you love. One of the fundamental fears in ROCD is *Will I get hurt if I let myself be vulnerable in this relationship?* This fear leads many people with relationship anxiety to be avoidant of deeper commitment and connection, including physical connection. That's because physical intimacy is quite possibly the most vulnerable we can be with another person; we are laid bare and exposed, our kinks, fantasies, and insecurities on display for possible scrutiny. Your anxiety has one mission—to protect you from this possibility at all costs—so it sends out intrusive images and racing thoughts that can make it feel impossible to get out of your head and into your body, the seat of desire and arousal.

Now take the inherent vulnerability of sex and mix in generations of religious and cultural stigma and repression. Add a tablespoon of media-fueled insecurity around your body, a dash of MOTO perfectionism around what sex *should* be like, and there you have it! A recipe for disaster in the bedroom. The distress that shows up in the way you kiss or the way you are being kissed—or the anxiety you feel when you imagine initiating sex or being on the receiving end of that initiation—is incredibly complex. It is the result of a convergence of religious, cultural, biological, and psychological factors, and though it might look effortless in the movies, the reality is that sex is a moral battleground and has been for centuries. Wherever the possibility of moral transgression lives, so too does anxiety. So you can imagine how untangling what we'll call *healthy sex* from this web of confusion takes a bit of effort and understanding, and it could take some time to achieve with your partner. And yet, MOTO boldly proclaims that if the connection between you and your partner is right, you should never have to work at it—generations of sociocultural conditioning be damned!

The truth is...

## Good Sex Is Hard Work

I find it interesting that while as a society we have some tolerance (though not a lot) for working on our relationships, we have almost none for our sex lives. What makes sex unique? Why would it be a relational arena exempt from attention, theory, and the application of tools and strategies? We keep sex locked in an airtight room and allow it to wither and die because we're so afraid of what we'll see if we bring it to the surface, so afraid of the stories our brain will tell us about our relationship and ourself if we venture into this space.

Oftentimes, a couple going through a sexual lull (every relationship has them) feels alone and uniquely flawed, but the truth is that so much of what my clients want to talk about in session, week after week, involves the details of their sex lives. They want to talk about what's normal, what's not, and how their ROCD makes it difficult to be intimate with the person they want the most. They feel suffocated by the expectation that sex should be effortless, passionate, and engaging throughout a lifetime and shamed by the belief that putting work in must mean that the chemistry just isn't there and never will be.

Nothing in a relationship can simply be set on autopilot, and yet sex, just like relationships, has been subsumed into the Myth of the One. We are told that chemistry and attraction should be instantaneous and that either a couple has a strong sexual connection or they don't—that there is no such thing as cultivating desire and good sex. According to MOTO, anything less than a perfect and uninterrupted connection spells disaster, so it's natural that your psychological watch dog (the amygdala) will be triggered by the weight of these expectations, sending out messages like *See! I told you this wasn't the right match. The connection just isn't there!*

MOTO wants you to believe:

- You should feel instant and immediate desire anytime your partner wants to have sex.

- You should like the way your partner touches you and shouldn't have to explain your turn ons/offs. They should just know.

- You should be having sex multiple times per week.

- The only thing that counts as real sex is intercourse.

- If you can't orgasm vaginally or if you require lubrication, it means your partner doesn't turn you on enough.

- You should always like the way your partner smells and tastes.

- You should never fantasize about anyone other than your partner.

- Sexual desire and interest should remain perfectly consistent over the course of a relationship.

You know I'm about to challenge all of this. But before we dive into what healthy sex actually looks like, it's important to note that, as with all the work in this book, none of what we discuss refers to any relationship or sex that is nonconsensual, violent, and disrespectful. None of our work should be applied to abusive or toxic relationships of any kind, where sex anxiety might have a very rational basis. Likewise, if you have experienced sexual trauma in the past or have been a victim of assault, then feelings of anxiety and fear around sex are a completely adaptive response, and your trauma deserves to be processed prior to working through this book.

If, however, you are in a fundamentally healthy and loving partnership, where mutual respect and desire exist, but just can't seem to feel comfortable, MOTO is a likely culprit. It is one thread of the complex web of factors that has fueled your sex anxiety, and it's where we'll start. Sex work is always deep and complex, and you shouldn't expect to solve this or any brand of anxiety overnight. However, by beginning to understand how the various factors exacerbate and inform your sex anxiety, you can initiate the process of freeing yourself from them; you will be taking the first important steps. The information in this chapter will help. If what you read here resonates with you and you want to learn more, I've included relevant resources in the back of this book to facilitate further exploration.

The first thing to know about healthy sex, is that…

## One Size Doesn't Fit All

It's tempting to want a clean definition of what healthy sex looks like so we can follow the rules perfectly and game the system, but certainty seeking is a trap. The truth is that healthy sex doesn't look one way; it isn't a one-size-fits-all phenomenon. Some days healthy sex might be wild and passionate like in the movies, while other days it might look like a cozy cuddle session on the couch. Healthy sex includes making love, and it includes quickies. It can include multiple partners, and it can include no partner, only yourself. That's because MOTO wants us to believe that the only kind of sex worth having involves two supermodels who reach simultaneous orgasm and never need a drop of lube to get there. MOTO wants us to believe that there's a valid way to be in a sexual relationship and an invalid way, and it definitely does not acknowledge that achieving and maintaining good sex, the healthy kind, is an arena that requires work and investment in the course of a long-term relationship.

In healthy sex, we realize:

- There is no such thing as the right amount of sex to have; there is only the amount and frequency that works for you and your partner.

- Your partner can't read your mind, so it's likely you will need to explain your turn ons/offs and communicate your needs and desires regularly.

- All forms of intimacy, including kissing, hugging, and masturbation, can be called sex—not just intercourse.

- Lubrication or the use of toys has nothing to do with how much you want or don't want sex with your partner and is not an indicator of your level of arousal.

- Fantasizing about other people is completely normal.

- Sexual desire waxes and wanes over time and is influenced by many factors, not just how attracted you are to your partner.

Like any other part of the human experience, your (and your partner's) levels of attraction, arousal, desire, and interest in sex are subject to flux and flow. They are affected by many factors. ROCD will say there is only one cause for anything less than mind-blowing MOTO sex multiple times per week: a lack of compatibility. But I've seen perfectly compatible couples who have sex once a month because that's the frequency that works for them and suits their needs. Likewise, I've seen couples who are intimate three times a week but still experience sex anxiety and want to work on the quality of their connection. And using lubrication or a vibrator to get out of your head and into the moment means nothing about your sexual chemistry, even though MOTO wants you to believe that any differences in your arousal level are because your partner just doesn't turn you on enough. This preposterous notion completely ignores the fact that physiological arousal (getting wet, turned on, erect) is often responsive and not spontaneous, a key distinction in our exploration of sex anxiety.

*Spontaneous arousal* describes the sudden, overwhelming need to have your partner and have them now—the brand of arousal we see in the movies that precedes sexual activity and can be ignited by a single touch. This arousal style can feel insatiable, instantaneous, and makes for great TV, and while it seems like everyone should be aroused in this way, studies show that 75 percent of men but only 15 percent of women describe having a spontaneous arousal style (Nagoski 2015). On the other hand, *responsive arousal* represents 5 percent of men and 30 percent of women and describes a "slow to warm" style. Whatever your gender identity or sexual orientation, if you are someone who has a responsive arousal style, you might not actively think about or want sex. But this doesn't mean you don't enjoy it! And it certainly doesn't mean something is wrong with you. It simply means that your body needs sexual cues in your environment to feel turned on. Responsive arousal activates *in response* to sexual things happening, like being touched, kissed, or desired by your partner. That's right! For many, sex is not a topic of interest unless it's actually happening.

Whether your style is responsive or spontaneous (or some combination, also normal) has little to do with sexual chemistry and everything to do with your biological and psychological makeup. It's so easy to feel shame about having a "low libido" when what's really happening is that you have a different style of arousal from your partner or from what the media say you should. It's also easy to feel like something must be wrong with you or your relationship when anxiety is blocking your access to desire and arousal—a connection we'll explore later in the chapter. This is why understanding what are completely normal variations in our biology and psychology can be powerful; when we discover how varied human sexuality is, we strip MOTO of its power and influence. You can then get to the work of discovering not what *should* work for you and your partner but what *does* work: what rhythm, toys, positions, schedule, and initiations suit your unique partnership. Learning what works for you and what works for you both can take some time, and it might not always be easy or comfortable. It certainly flies in the face of the MOTO myth of perfect ease and effortlessness. But the investment you put into uncovering and celebrating your unique connection is exactly what healthy sex is all about. One size does not fit all.

## Fantasy Is Normal

Every single day, we are educated on what good sex should look and feel like, not by a therapist or a doctor, but through our surrogate sex instructor—the media. The barrage of misinformation is overwhelming, with studies finding that sexual content, whether implicit or explicit, appears in 85 percent of the movies and 82 percent of the TV shows we watch every single day (Ward et al. 2016). The list of unrealistic expectations we are presented with is endless, but there are a few lies that warrant particular attention, ones that I see so often in treatment they deserve their time in the spotlight. Among them is the notion that if you are with the right partner, you shouldn't ever fantasize about being with someone else and that doing so is a relationship red flag or, even worse, tantamount to betrayal.

The science, however, just doesn't support this, with studies showing that a whopping 80 percent of women and 98 percent of men having fantasized about having sex with someone other than their current partner (Hicks and Leitenberg 2001). That's a hugely significant number, one that shows that it's far rarer not to fantasize than it is to do so! And yet you might be very anxious about what fantasy means about your relationship and level of sexual satisfaction. That's because MOTO will have us believe that the content of our fantasies represents our secret desires and that whomever we fantasize about is the one we really want to be with or the kind of person we really want to be. MOTO tells us that fantasy in the context of a monogamous relationship is morally transgressive and that those who fantasize are bad people in the wrong relationships.

Framing fantasy as morally transgressive is wildly inaccurate and massively anxiety producing. Worse, it robs us of fantasy's true purpose— to be an arena of imaginative play and exploration, one that adds vitality and energy to your sexual relationship rather than detracts from it. In our fantasies we have space to safely explore other options and identities without jeopardizing our primary relationship; we can play make-believe for a night without ever needing to step outside!

My clients have confessed that they fantasize about sex with cowork- ers, married friends, and people they pass on the street. They describe same-sex fantasies, fantasies of domination and submission, and even fantasies of rape. Many worry about the implications of these fantasies, asking, "Does this mean I'm in denial of my true sexuality? Am I a hor- rible person who gets turned on by hurting people?" or, "What if this fantasy means I'm no longer in love with my partner?" So I tell them what I'll tell you, that your fantasy can stay in the realm of imagination forever, if you want it to, and that the content of that fantasy doesn't necessarily mean anything about what you would actually like to do in the light of day. You may choose to let your fantasy play out in your rela- tionship (as long as your partner is willing), or you can just enjoy it all by yourself—it's absolutely up to you!

The beauty of fantasy is it can be a vehicle for exploration, connec- tion, and enjoyment, allowing you to explore a world of possibility within the structure of your relationship. Of course, like all things, fantasy can also become compulsive. If you notice that you are fantasizing about other people every time you're intimate with your partner or using fantasy to ignore real issues in the relationship that feel too scary to address, then you will want to reexamine it. You also will want to be careful not to act out what-if intrusive thoughts and confuse this for fantasy. Anxiously checking *Am I more aroused by the thought of being with my coworker than by the thought of being with my partner? Let me check!* is a compulsion that fuels ROCD and can create more distance in your relationship. If you notice that you are engaged in an unhealthy relationship with fantasy and are using it as compulsive escapism, further exploration is warranted. But for the overwhelming majority of my ROCD clients, fantasy is just another piece of healthy sexuality MOTO has convinced them is dangerous; it is yet another lie they must untangle and set straight.

## Choose Quality over Quantity

Another myth worth debunking is that sex should happen multiple times per week and that less frequent sex is a sign of danger or impending doom in your relationship. We have been told that there is a right amount of sex to have and a wrong amount, so it makes sense that you might find yourself anxious if you ever fall below the MOTO mark. But this fixation on hitting a sex quota completely disregards the quality of the sex being had. It entirely ignores the much more important question of whether or not sex—be it oral sex, manual sex, masturbation, or intimacy of any kind—is pleasurable and serves to create or maintain connection between you and your partner.

Moreover, fixating on quantity rather than quality ignores our fundamental humanness. It's blind to the fact that you and your partner are real people who experience stress and transition, that there will always be seasons of greater intimacy and those of less connection, and that no arena of human life is perfectly consistent. It makes the robotic assumption that a couple should be having the same amount of sex after having children—while navigating sickness or loss of health and through times of work or family stress—as they did before, though stress is all but guaranteed to shut down desire and snuff out libido. Put simply, the number of times you have sex is not an accurate indicator of relational health. And when we measure our relationships by the quantity standard, we disregard the truth: that it is far better to have sex the number of times per week, month, or year that suits your unique partnership and to enjoy the sex that you *do* have than to allow MOTO to dictate your pace.

By challenging what MOTO says sex should be like (*Wild! Passionate! Mind-blowing every time!*) and adopting a more balanced view (understanding sex is context-dependent, complex, and different with each partner), your anxiety will have less fuel to burn. You'll come to see that so much of what you worry is a sign of incompatibility is actually perfectly normal. And while I can't promise that your sex anxiety is purely the result of the factors explored in this chapter (we don't deal in certainty, remember?), I can tell you that MOTO misinformation doesn't make things any easier. When you release the impossible standards that have been placed on your sex life, you open space for true intimacy to flourish. You begin to see your partner for who they really are, not for who they should be, and from this space, you can cultivate what healthy sex means to you, the only opinion that truly matters.

**EXERCISE:** Grab a journal or notebook and list the MOTO messages you have internalized about what good sex should look and feel like. Then review this list and consider which messages you want to release. Ask yourself, *Does holding on to this message create more connection and intimacy in my relationship or more distance and anxiety?*

## Sex, Sin, and Anxiety

Clearly, MOTO has got to go. Ditching its damaging messages will significantly diminish your sex anxiety. But doing this will take some effort. This brand of anxiety has very deep roots that go back centuries and are as much a part of the human story as any ancient church or mosque. Healing sex anxiety can feel so loaded because when you begin to explore it, you realize you're not just challenging the Hollywood myth of perfection, but also pushing against deep messaging about what it means to be pure, good, and desirable. You realize you're up against some seriously old-school messaging about what it means to be a worthy member of society.

A common thread in those with OCD and anxiety is a keen eye for honesty and a desire to be moral. In fact, the first documented case of what we now call OCD was described by a bishop in the seventeenth century who noticed a member of his clergy so tortured by a fear of sinning that he engaged in hours of daily rituals to cleanse his soul and become worthy of redemption. While the content of our obsessions may shift, the search for truth in OCD remains a unifying thread. Sometimes that search morphs into *hypermorality*, which is an exaggerated and compulsive need to be virtuous, honest, and good by society's standards.

Sex anxiety is certainly fueled by MOTO perfectionism, but it is also powered by the fear that by opening up sexually we will violate certain social standards and thus be seen as morally transgressive. We worry that by dropping our inhibitions we will be found out as deviant or sick, and thus rejected, cast out of connection and belonging. One way to avoid this rejection (according to your ROCD) is to never get too close, to never become vulnerable enough to allow another person to see your desires, fantasies, and kinks, the very parts that could lead to social censure. *Keep a safe distance emotionally and physically!* ROCD argues. *It's the only way to be certain others won't actually find out how abnormal you really are!*

Unfortunately, it's also the best way to snuff out your sex life.

When deciding what to judge as morally transgressive, your ROCD has a torrent of messages to choose from. That's because sex and sexuality have been regulated by religion, culture, and society for thousands of years—reigned in and controlled by those who fear it. Even in modern times, those of us who identify as women grow up hearing that sex before marriage is a sin and that overt expressions of sexuality are reprehensible. We are told that to be overly sexual detracts from our credibility, but to be undersexual is a sign of frigidity. Women are told that they should celebrate their bodies, but not too much lest they be provocative. That they shouldn't have too many sexual partners because that means they are slutty. But wait! Too few sexual partners makes you a prude, so avoid that too.

Sex educator and author Emily Nagoski discusses this maddening confusion when she says, "We're raising women to be sexually dysfunctional, with all the 'no' messages we're giving them about diseases and shame and fear. And then as soon as they're eighteen, they're supposed to be sexual rock stars, multiorgasmic and totally uninhibited. It doesn't make any sense. None of the things we do in our society prepares women for that" (2015, 155).

Women have historically been on the receiving end of these damaging messages. But those who identify as men are also taught to believe that they need to be up for and always ready for sex. They have been told that their ability to achieve an erection is as central to their manhood as their ability to contain their emotions, and that their sexual worth is based on partner count and penis size. This is an equally damaging narrative, which shuts down a man's complex inner world and reduces him to the role of a superficial initiator. It often leads to difficulty achieving and maintaining arousal too. Contrary to popular belief, most men not only want to have sex, but also want to feel seen, accepted, and desired. And like women, men can get so caught up in what they should and shouldn't do that there is no space left for true sexual enjoyment and connection. With all these conflicting messages, it's no wonder that sex can feel impossible. *I give up!* anxiety says. *The best way to stay safe and ensure I'm not rejected is to shut down desire and forgo intimacy altogether. The stakes just feel too high.*

## Why Desire Can Feel So Dangerous

It can be tempting to blame ourselves for what isn't working in the bedroom and then to transfer that blame onto our partners or relationships. But the truth is that anxiety shuts down desire. It shuts down attraction, it shuts down arousal, and it shuts down orgasm. It shuts down all your erotic inroads in an attempt to keep you safe from the complexity of sex and the possibility of rejection. Navigating this maze of moral messaging without losing your libido can feel impossible, and it can feel anything but romantic to engage sexually when it seems like your reputation is on the line. Guilt and shame, after all, make terrible aphrodisiacs.

Many of my clients describe a fear around initiating sex. Many find being on the receiving end much easier than expressing genuine desire toward their partner. Given the minefield of morality that sex has become, it makes sense that desiring your partner can feel uncomfortable at best and dangerous at worst. When we express desire, we give our partner the power to reject us. We strip down physically and emotionally, hoping they look at us and like whom they see, hoping that they accept us and meet our vulnerability with their own.

By initiating sex, you encounter the possibility not just of a rejection in the moment, but of a wholehearted rejection of who you are, a repudiation of your deepest self. In Nathaniel Hawthorne's classic American novel, *The Scarlett Letter,* Hester Prynn is shunned from her Puritan society for the sin of adultery. Forced to wear a scarlet A (for adulterer) at all times, she becomes, as novelist John Updike says, "an epitome of female predicaments": "a mythic version of every woman's attempt to integrate her sexuality with societal demands" (Seabrook 2008).

*The Scarlett Letter* was written over 150 years ago, yet one need not look far to see the same puritanical influences today. And whatever your sexual orientation and gender identity, the challenge remains the same for you as it does for Hester Prynn: how to be fully alive and uninhibited sexually in a culture that still fears and regulates that expression. How to fully integrate your sexual self with your morally upstanding self, how to be nice and naughty all at once. Given this challenge, desire can feel anything but easy or light; in fact, it can feel outright rebellious!

Of course, it was never your responsibility to shoulder this burden in the first place. Your sexuality should never have been a sacrificial lamb for the social, cultural, and religious pressures that have distorted it from a pure expression of aliveness into what it is today. Our overview of culture and how it contributes to sex anxiety in this chapter is merely an introduction to an extraordinarily complex history, one that warrants further exploration and understanding. But the simple takeaway is that living in and being socialized in a society that stigmatizes full sexual expression breeds anxiety and stifles desire. Enthusiastic arousal in the middle of this moral minefield is completely unrealistic, and yet we constantly blame ourselves and judge our relationships when we don't feel perfectly turned on.

But how exactly does anxiety shut down sexual desire?

## How Anxiety Blocks Arousal

The key to understanding the biological relationship between anxiety and arousal lies in understanding the dual control model (DCM) of sexual response, a theory developed by John Bancroft and Erick Janssen in the late 1990s (Bancroft et al. 2009). According to this theory, human desire is broken up into two main processes, the activation of the accelerator and the pumping of the brakes. The accelerator is called the sexual excitation system (SES) and is constantly scanning the environment for sexual cues through your senses of sight, smell, sound, taste, and touch, ready to tell your system to *turn on* for the possibility of sex. If it receives the *go* signal, the SES sends input from your brain to your genitals to get you going, beginning the arousal process. If you've ever watched a movie with a sex scene and noticed the slight tingling of arousal, that's the SES turning up and tuning in. The SES never turns off, humming just below your awareness like a car idling at the start of a race, always ready for a green light.

On the other hand, the sexual inhibition system (SIS) is like the brakes of the car, which also receive input from the environment. However, the job of the SIS is to find any reason *not* to become aroused, to identify any factors that might make having sex unsafe or unwanted. The SIS notices any potential threats in your external or internal environment and sends the *turn off* signal to your body, engaging the brakes and slowing down or shutting off your desire and libido. "All sexual functioning and all sexual dysfunction," Nagoski writes, "is a balance (or imbalance) between brakes and accelerator" (2015, 50). You might have already guessed it, but anxiety is a lead weight slamming down on the brakes of your car. Even with a sensitive accelerator (someone with a high sex drive), if the brakes are on, you won't be going very far.

Below are a few reasons your brakes could get triggered:

- Negative body image and poor self-esteem

- Concerns about reputation and stigma, for example, fear of being "bad" or "slutty"

- Worries about pregnancy

- Painful sex

- Feeling used by a partner instead of wanted

- Intrusive thoughts about your partner or relationship

- Feeling tired, stressed, or overwhelmed

- Concerns about sexually transmitted infections

- Low mood, feelings of depression, and worry

As an anxious person, you are already hyperattuned to any perceived threats in your environment, so when the brakes of your arousal system feel even the slightest bit triggered by any of the fears listed above, for example, *What if I'm not into this and my partner can tell?* or *What if I don't like the way they are touching me?* your brakes will engage. But rather than a gentle tap that could allow you to stay in the moment, something like *I don't need to be 100 percent into this yet. Let me go with it and see what happens,* ROCD causes you to slam down hard on the brakes and can halt desire and arousal altogether. If you've ever been the passenger of a nervous driver, you have an idea of what this is like. Maybe the driver sees a dog on the sidewalk and, rather than slowing slightly, slams on the brakes preemptively, making the ride stilted and uncomfortable.

Everyone's gas pedal (what turns them on) and brakes (what turns them off) are unique to them and the result of a multitude of factors like past sexual experiences, genetics, and environment, and having strong brakes is nothing to be ashamed of. There is also no such thing as a normal combination of accelerator and brakes, and what turns one person on could very well turn another off. But it's fair to say that unhelpful MOTO messaging doesn't make you any less lead footed. It's also fair to say that untangling yourself from the cultural, religious, and societal stories you have been fed about your sexuality is key to becoming a smoother driver. Challenging the notion that there's a right and wrong way to do things gives your brain fewer reasons to tap the brakes and many more opportunities to become a confident driver in the raceway of desire.

Sometimes, gaining that confidence requires that you push the gas pedal even when you're scared to do so. And there are times when you might decide to be intimate even when that's the last thing your anxiety wants you to do. Most everyone will tell you that you should only engage with a romantic partner when you're 100 percent comfortable and certain, but I disagree. If you have an anxiety disorder, there is a time to step into connection, even when you're not feeling absolutely certain you want to. That is, there's a time to take your foot off the brakes and push the accelerator even when you're nervous to do so, even if you're not 100 percent sure you'll be into it or if your partner is The One. That's because the anxiety you experience in ROCD is often a false alarm, a threat response that can't always be trusted to guide you where you want to go in life. It also means that waiting for 100 percent certainty that you are ready—whether to commit to your partner, to say "I love you," or to initiate sex and intimacy—might mean you'll wait forever.

This "fake it till you make it" mentality works in the treatment of anxiety of all kinds because it combats our need to be 100 percent certain we have the right feelings before proceeding. In sex anxiety, that means gently pushing through MOTO messaging, sociocultural baggage, and sensitive brakes: taking a leap of faith to see that although vulnerability is indeed scary, it can also be safe and even exhilarating. Of course, sex should never be forced or rushed in any way, and the best partners are those who can respect whatever pace you need to work through your anxiety, slowly and gently. But if you wait to feel perfectly ready or perfectly certain of your emotions before taking that leap of faith, your anxiety will win by keeping you distant. It wins by keeping you safe but ultimately disconnected from intimacy and love.

## Sex Is Complicated (and That's a Good Thing!)

If you're a little confused at this point, then we're on track. The reality of sex is a complicated one, and the only way to free yourself from this complexity is to honor it. The way to break out of the landslide of expectations and unrealistic messaging fueling your sex anxiety and ROCD is to see how every sexual experience is uniquely different, and that there is no one right way to do it, only the right way for you and your partner. You've been told good sex should be easy and effortless, and that anything else is a problem with you or with your relationship, just like you've been conditioned to feel that anxiety in a relationship clearly means you've made a mistake. But the truth is that good sex can be hard, it can be messy, and it is *always* an arena of immense vulnerability. Sex is a meeting point of cultural, biological, and psychological factors that make it uniquely charged and especially prone to becoming a source of anxiety and conflict in a relationship. Healthy sex is complicated. Anyone who tells you otherwise is probably trying to manipulate your power.

Healthy sex isn't just something that happens when you find the right relationship or the perfect match; it is the product of time and investment. There isn't a one-size-fits-all solution to achieving and maintaining it, and comparison is futile because every single person and partnership is different. To top it all off, none of the work you invest guarantees that you won't sometimes feel the pain of vulnerability or that your partner won't one day reject you and break your heart. Yup! Sex is complicated. While the complexity might scare you, my hope is that it will also set you free. By recognizing that there is no such thing as the right way (but only *your* way), you can turn your attention away from what sex *should* look like and focus more on how to connect with the person you love, the one you have chosen.

We've covered plenty of information in the first few chapters of this book, and right about now, you might be itching to put it all to use, to harness what you've learned about relationship anxiety, sex anxiety, and ROCD into real tools and strategies for healing. In the next few chapters, we'll do exactly that. We will move past the question of *Why do I feel this block in my romantic relationship?* and into a step-by-step solution for how to address your anxiety and cultivate the kind of love and connection you've always wanted. In doing so, you'll nudge past the absolute need to know if you've made the right decision and step more fully into the unknown—cultivating a place to stand in that feared space.

The truth is that, in love as in life, there's no way to be 100 percent certain. We cannot be entirely safe and live fully at the same time, just as we cannot fully love without the possibility of loss; all true adventures involve encounters with uncertainty. Ultimately, my hope is that you'll come to see the version of safety your anxiety offers for what it really is: a weak substitute for the powerful freedom that awaits you on the other side of fear.

You just need to know the way forward.

# PART 2

# Rewiring Your Anxious Brain

# CHAPTER 4

# Cognitive Distortions and Thought Restructuring

If you're reading this book, it's likely that you want a meaningful and fulfilling partnership, and it's likely that fear and anxiety are keeping you from fully committing to the person you have chosen. This fear, the gut-wrenching pain that blocks your ability to connect, might seem impossible to track, let alone treat. It might feel entirely ingrained and completely habitual. But your brain and its patterns are far more predictable and changeable than you might think. Yes, ROCD is clever and finds plenty of ways to get your attention, but anxious thinking also tends to follow recognizable patterns that we can track, challenge, and ultimately dismantle. You spent the first few chapters gaining a deeper understanding of what fear and anxiety in a good partnership can look like. Now let's explore how to overcome it.

## How You Are Wired

You might get tired of hearing this, but your brain is an incredible machine. It takes in millions of stimuli and pieces of information from your environment every minute and sorts through this data to produce the thoughts and feelings that help you efficiently navigate your world and stay alive. The actual numbers are incredible; our senses gather about eleven million bits of information per second, sending these bits to the brain with lightning speed so that we have all the information needed to avoid falling off a cliff or getting attacked by a potential predator. Even though the human brain is only able to process about fifty bits out of the eleven million per second that enter it, this incredible adaptation has allowed us to evolve into the dominant (and destructive) species we are today.

No doubt about it, the human brain can do amazing things. But with all that information coming in, how do we organize and decide what pieces are most important? How do our brains decide what warrants a reaction (*Run! Attack! Hide!*), and what stimulus goes in the discard? Through shortcuts, of course! These shortcuts usually work quite well, allowing us to navigate life with shocking ease and alacrity. It goes something like this: you know exactly how to tie a shoe. You also know that every category of sneaker, be it white, athletic, or high-top, needs to be tied. And in your brain, the shoe-tying wires have already been connected and generalized, so when you put on any sneaker, your brain automatically knows that *sneaker* = *tie*. You don't need to waste even a moment thinking about how to do this complicated procedure; your brain just generalizes, and off you go! For the most part, this evolutionary organization tool works wonderfully, allowing us to perform complex tasks like driving or preparing our morning coffee without a second thought. When functioning correctly, mental shortcuts help us navigate our world and free up our attention so that we can focus on much more important things.

But sometimes, the brain's superpowered ability to make these connections and shortcuts goes too far, overgeneralizing when it should be more nuanced. You might experience this as a feeling of threat or danger where there really is none, and automatically jump from the thought *There is a small chance this could be a problem* to the thought *Danger! Get out!* In psychology, we call these unhelpful shortcuts *cognitive distortions*, and if you have an anxiety disorder, it's likely your brain has gotten a bit too good at drawing conclusions. It's as if your brain were to apply the command *tie the shoe* not only to sneakers but to heels, sandals, and flats. There are simply more categories of shoes that need to be accounted for, and not all shoes must be tied. And in relationship anxiety, rather than registering the important nuances of a relationship, rather than recognizing that some things are sneakers while others are stilettos, your brain has a tendency to jump straight to the worst-case scenario.

Cognitive distortions are tricky because they form so automatically throughout the day that, for the most part, we're not even aware that we're making these unhelpful generalizations. This lack of awareness is generally fine as long as the wiring upstairs aligns with reality, allowing you to see the world rationally and to assess threat clearly. But if you're reading this book, it's likely you've been wired by genetics and environment to fear connection, intimacy, and vulnerability. It's likely your brain generalizes these fears in ways you might not even be aware of, in ways that could be negatively affecting your relationship. Your brain could be taking a few too many shortcuts, confusing, for example, *all* relationships with pain and *all* doubt with danger. If you notice that your brain is a little too good at jumping to these kinds of conclusions, it might be time for a little rewiring.

The good news is that there is absolutely a way to rewire faulty thinking, to catch and correct these shortcuts and manually balance them out in our minds. Through this more balanced lens, your anxiety will have less to react to because nuance in a situation naturally takes down the heat. The gray area can be uncomfortable, but it is clearly less drama than the black-and-white nature of most distorted cognitions. And from this more balanced perspective, you might then find it easier to relax into vulnerability, connection, and intimacy and, thus, into love.

## Common Cognitive Distortions

To begin balancing your perspective and color correcting your lens to gray, let's start by looking at the six most common cognitive distortions in ROCD. We'll also explore how to use some tools from cognitive behavioral therapy to go about correcting them.

# 1. All-or-Nothing Thinking

*All-or-nothing thinking* is viewing a situation in black-and-white terms instead of seeing the gray areas or a continuum.

> *Janel, a young mother who's been married for five years, has recently been troubled by recurring thoughts she's been having about her ex, a man she had dated throughout her early twenties but ultimately left. The trouble started as she was scrolling through Facebook and saw a picture of her ex and his new wife. Ever since, she's been having dreams about what her life could have been like if she had chosen to stay with him and how it might feel to run into him again and maybe even fall back in love. Janel is terrified that these dreams are meaningful and point to the terrifying possibility that she is no longer satisfied with her partner. She worries that the only way to feel good again is to separate, split up her family, and start a new life altogether.*

Janel is firmly caught in a cognitive distortion called all-or-nothing thinking, where the brain speeds past the gray areas and lands right in a worst-case conclusion, where it takes a shortcut from A (thought) to Z (worst-case scenario). Her shortcut says that dreams about anyone other than her partner are dangerous and that fantasies are clear signs of dissatisfaction. But this mental shortcut is no longer serving Janel, because it misses the deeper truth: that you can have pleasurable thoughts about an ex while still loving your current partner, and that fantasies don't necessarily say anything about your true preferences or desires. The all-or-nothing lens is a rigid one that offers only two options: black or white, good or bad, success or failure. And for Janel, either she is totally in love, free of any doubts, or her relationship must be doomed. This distortion traps us in a binary and rigid view of the world around us and of our relationships, one that leaves little room for the gray area where the truth so often resides.

Of course, many of your thoughts are important, meaningful, and worthy of attention. So how do you know which to listen to and which are simply an exaggeration of the anxious mind? You don't actually have to answer this question. You don't need to know for sure if your thoughts are rational or not, and you don't need to catch every single thought your brain sends your way with 100 percent success. You only need to add one additional step between having a thought and automatically believing it. You need to run your relationship-based thinking through a filter, one that's meant to ensure you don't jump straight from white to black, from good to bad, and from doubt to disaster; one that brings out the gray area in any situation, balancing the colors. So the next time you hear an all-or-nothing distortion in your thoughts, remind yourself that this isn't the only way to think.

**Response:** "This is all-or-nothing thinking. Just because [triggering thought or event], this does not automatically mean [horrible conclusion]. Thoughts don't necessarily equal facts."

## 2. Catastrophizing

Also known as fortune telling, *catastrophizing* is seeing a situation to its worst-case conclusion in the future.

*Chris has recently returned to treatment after a long hiatus, reporting a desire to tackle his newest ROCD obsession, one that has caused many fights and sleepless nights in the past few months of his relationship. Chris and his partner, James, have been together for more than a decade, and the two live a life filled with travel and late-night socializing. But lately, James has been bringing up the idea of starting a family, triggering a tremendous amount of anxiety and panic in Chris. "I love James, and when we met, both of us said we wanted kids. But now that it's actually a reality to consider, all I can think about is how having a child will be the end of my life as I know it," he explains. "I'll lose all my freedom, and we'll end up boring and sexless just like our parent friends. James will see what a bad parent I am and eventually leave me! Nothing will ever be the same again. I just know it!"*

It's easy for me to see why Chris is so anxious. His brain believes it can predict the future, and from what he can tell, the future doesn't look too inviting.

Catastrophizing is characterized by a chain-like spiral of thinking (and then this will happen, and then, and then) that quickly moves from one horrible conclusion to the next, all the way to a catastrophic future outcome. In this distortion, your brain takes the possibility of future pain and expresses it as fact, leaving you overwhelmed and terrified in the face of what sounds like an inevitable disaster. Catastrophizing jacks up our anxiety in two ways. First, it magnifies the likelihood of the feared outcome occurring (loss of autonomy leads to sexlessness, which leads to divorce). Then, it minimizes our trust in our ability to cope with that outcome if it were to happen. And the bigger the catastrophe, the less capable we feel to tolerate it! Enter anxiety.

Much like in the previous example of all-or-nothing thinking, the goal of challenging catastrophizing isn't to tell yourself *That won't ever happen,* because we really don't know for sure; we can't predict the future. What we can do is notice when our brain is fortune telling and step back into the gray area, into the balance of the unknown. And while Chris swears that he knows exactly how things would unfold if James and he were to have kids, he doesn't. He can't possibly know what will happen or how they will feel. He can't predict the future.

The truth is that while it's unlikely that Chris's horror story would unfold exactly as his brain says it would, if becoming a parent really did complicate his marriage, he would still have options. They could try couples therapy to better navigate the toll on their relationship. Chris could hire a babysitter and invest time in his own hobbies and interests to regain his autonomy. Or, worst-case scenario, he could choose to leave his relationship while continuing to coparent with James. The point is, he has options, and no matter how challenging it would be, if Chris chose to, he could cope with every single worst-case outcome. He could choose to go on and have a meaningful life, no matter what his anxiety may tell him. And if Chris can cope, then so can you. You've just got to remind yourself that you can, whenever you find yourself caught up in dwelling on the worst-case scenario.

**Response:** "I'm catastrophizing right now. I can't predict what will happen in the future, and no matter what happens, I could choose to cope with the outcome."

## 3. Emotional Reasoning

*Emotional reasoning* is believing something is true simply because you feel it so strongly, even when all the evidence points in a different direction.

> *Joel has been dating Leona for months but swears he can't commit to seeing her exclusively. He says this even though they spend most days of the week together, have great sex, and share many interests and hobbies. And yet, he's not sure he can take the next step. That's because for Joel, this is a new kind of relationship; Leona isn't anything like the more casual flings he typically enters into, and she has been clear with Joel that she's serious and isn't looking to play games. "Leona is the kind of woman I've always seen myself with," he says. "I'd like to commit, but the truth is that sometimes when I look at her, I just feel so turned off. Like she's disgusting or even repulsive to me sometimes. How can this not mean it's all wrong?" He struggles to reconcile these confusing feelings with the otherwise positive ones he generally experiences toward Leona and toward the relationship.*

Like you, Joel has grown up in a culture that elevates the notion of trusting your gut to the status of divine direction. So when Joel feels disgust and even repulsion toward Leona, he's convinced something must be terribly wrong with their relationship. His gut sometimes (but not always) sends messages of disinterest, so they must be true, right? Not always. While trusting your gut might be helpful in other arenas of your life, if you have relationship anxiety, *you must disregard this advice when assessing your partnership.* Remember the talk we had about butterflies in chapter 1? How butterflies are anticipatory fear signals from your amygdala, and that they can't be trusted to indicate whether or not your relationship is actually a good one? Well, that gut feeling is exactly the same sort of thing.

When you're scared, be it of a flight across the country, an upcoming test, or the possibility of being vulnerable in your relationship, you will notice plenty of gut feelings arise. They may tell you the plane will surely crash, that you will surely fail, or that the person you're dating is surely not The One. But what we *feel* to be true is frequently a more accurate indicator of what we *fear* to be true than a clear marker of the truth itself. And that's because many of the feelings in your gut are produced by none other than (drum roll) the amygdala! That's right, it's the part of the brain that misfires in OCD and other anxiety disorders, the portion responsible for sending out messages of threat. And, fascinatingly, research has shown that disgust and anxiety are related emotional experiences (Cisler et al. 2009). Feelings of disgust and aversion might mean you're not liking what's happening, or they could mean you're just scared of what's happening. So perhaps Joel is less disgusted by Leona than he is afraid of what she represents: a journey into love but also into the possibility of pain, rejection, and abandonment.

This does not mean we throw out emotions altogether; they serve as valuable data points to be considered when making important decisions in our lives. But it does mean that before you believe that whatever you feel is important and factual, you must run your emotion through the same filter that you've been using to correct all-or-nothing thinking and catastrophizing—to make sure that what you feel as intuition isn't just a fear response keeping you from good love. Joel might very well decide in the end that he doesn't want to pursue a relationship with Leona, because he just doesn't have the sort of feelings he needs to move forward. But by correcting his lens and running his emotions through our filter, he will be making that decision based on real evidence, not just a fleeting gut feeling. The next time you notice an anxious feeling and confuse this with truth, try reminding yourself of this.

**Response:** "Just because I feel something doesn't automatically make it true. Feelings don't always equal facts."

## 4. Should or Must Statements (Perfectionism)

Another cognitive distortion involves having precise, fixed, and unrealistic ideas about our lives, relationships, or feelings. Such *should* or *must statements* are also known as perfectionism.

> *Growing up, Rahel's parents appeared to have it all figured out when it came to marriage and love. She never saw them fight or argue and says that they were so in sync they appeared practically able to read one another's minds. She knew from a young age exactly what she wanted a relationship to look like: she would never settle for less than magic, for less than the perfect love she saw her parents share.*
>
> *But a recently married Rahel worries she has done just that. She tells me that she and her husband disagree, misunderstand one another, and that sometimes loving him doesn't feel easy. She worries this is all a sign that she's made a huge mistake. "Some days I feel totally in love and connected! But other times all I want is space. Those are the days I don't feel any desire or love, and to be honest, those are the days I fantasize about what it would be like if I were single again." Rahel finds herself fixating on her partner's flaws hours per day, ruminating on all the ways their marriage falls short of her picture-perfect ideal.*

Can we blame Rahel for wanting a perfect relationship? She's been raised on MOTO messaging that's been magnified by her parents' own seemingly perfect marriage. She's heard in a thousand different ways what an ideal relationship should look and feel like, and now believes that the presence of bad days in her marriage must mean something is terribly wrong. Of course, she has no knowledge of what the early days of her parents' relationship were like or what truly happens behind closed doors in their partnership. But her brain will overlook that detail because

Rahel is stuck in the distortion of perfectionism. She has come to believe that all good relationships must share the same qualities and that days of disconnection, times of misunderstanding, and a desire for alone time have no place in true love. *I shouldn't feel this way*, perfectionism says. *If I do, something must be wrong.*

Do we ever pause to consider the standards we are holding ourselves to and assess whether they actually serve us? Do we take the time to pause and consider if, by searching to either be or find the perfect person, we're not missing out on the real thing right in front of us, the good-enough thing? We lose so much when we try to sanitize our humanity and purify our thoughts. We lose so much in the pursuit of perfection. And much like the OCD client who washes their hands until they feel perfectly clean, perfectionism causes us to wash our relationships dry. We go past a good-enough clean and sanitize our relationships, so badly do we desire all the right thoughts and all the right feelings in love.

After all, what's wrong with a good-enough clean? And what's wrong with good-enough love? The concept of *good enough* may offend your romantic sensibilities, but it's exactly the right solution for the perfectionist inside us all. The truth is that when we try to remove every speck of dirt from our relationships, we sterilize them. Ultimately, perfectionism is a form of protection, a psychological defense meant to save us from the messiness of what it means to live and to love, to get our hands dirty in the game of life, because, no matter how hard we may try, human imperfection simply can't be washed away. We'll talk all about our wonderful messiness in chapter 7 (when we explore shame and ROCD), but for now, just notice when your brain sends you should and must statements. Notice when your brain is gunning for perfection and gently correct it with this response.

**Response:** "These standards are unrealistic. Neither my partner nor our relationship has to be 100 percent perfect all the time, and neither do I. Good enough is good enough!"

## 5. Comparison

Comparing your life, relationship, or level of struggle to another person's, when you really don't know the whole story, is another cognitive distortion.

*Usman is two months away from his wedding date, and every day, it seems, his friends and family members ask him about his relationship. They want to know if he's excited to be taking this next step in his life, and can't seem to let the questions drop. But Usman's feelings are mixed—he loves his fiancée very much but is terrified of change and transition, of the unknown and what it really means to be married and committed for life. Sometimes Usman compares his level of happiness to couples on social media, and other times he compares himself to the people around him. He wonders if his partner and he are in love enough, affectionate enough, or compatible enough and spends hours wondering if others have it all figured out while he's just lying to himself. Usman tries to gain certainty about the rightness of his own relationship by looking at the relationships around him and finds himself caught in endless checking and reassurance seeking as he tries to solve the question "Do I love her enough to take the next step?"*

Every single person you know falls into the trap of comparison at times because it's hardwired into our core nature to compare ourselves to those around us. This tendency to compare comes from our evolutionary history in tribal communities where fitting in with the group was literally a matter of life or death. Strong social connections were what kept our ancestors alive; if you didn't measure up, you could be expelled from the security of the tribe and left to fend for yourself in the wilderness. Over millennia, humans evolved to place a massive emphasis on social standing and social connection, and so we continue to compare ourselves to those around us. Today, the difference is that we can compare ourselves not to members of a small tribe, whose lives we are intimately aware of and intertwined with, but to people we've never met. Now we have social media, where it's shockingly easy to feel like our lives and relationships are inadequate even if we know what we're seeing is mostly fake and filtered.

But what about real-life relationships? Usman has plenty of couples around him, be it friends or acquaintances, who also trigger his anxiety and make him feel that what he and his fiancée have might not be true love. Some of his friends seem more infatuated than he is, some more confident in their relationships. Some of his friends have more objectively beautiful partners or ones who seem to laugh at all their jokes, never taking offense like Usman's fiancée sometimes does. But what we see on the outside is often barely representative of the complexities of another person's life or love story. And even if you know someone intimately, it's still difficult to make an accurate comparison. Even more importantly, the qualities that work for and draw together another couple might never have worked for you! Every couple has their own love story, their own compatible and incompatible points, their own struggles. No matter how tempting it may be to draw comparisons, the assumed happiness of others is far too tenuous a way to judge something as important as the quality of your relationship.

There is no such thing as a perfect template for love. All partnership is a collaboration; it is a story you and your partner write together, one that has never been written before and will never be written again. One size doesn't fit all. So the next time you notice yourself making comparisons, remind yourself of this.

**Response:** "I have absolutely no idea what another person's life or relationship is truly like."

## 6. Mind Reading

Believing you know what other people are thinking, without considering other, more likely alternatives, is known as *mind reading*.

*Ada came to therapy consumed with thoughts that she was not truly loved by her girlfriend, whom she had been dating for six months. "She says she loves me, but that doesn't stop my brain from asking the question a thousand times a day! I ask her for reassurance constantly, and even though she swears she adores me, I just look at her and can't help but think she's over it." But Ada's girlfriend has shown no signs of wanting to leave the relationship. On the contrary, she has committed to attending couples therapy with Ada in hopes of learning how better to support Ada as she manages her anxiety and OCD. She gives constant reassurance and does anything to quell Ada's fears of unlovability. But it's never enough, and Ada just can't seem to escape the intrusive thought that her girlfriend is growing cold and will eventually leave her because "I am an anxious and emotional mess."*

Mind reading is a cognitive shortcut that projects our own fears onto the thoughts of others and, in the absence of real evidence, often assumes the worst. If you've ever been at a party and felt like everyone was talking about a blemish on your face or an awkward thing you said, only to find out later that no one even noticed, you've experienced this distortion and know just how convincing it can seem in the moment. In ROCD, this can manifest as a tendency to mind-read our own partner or to mind-read how others around us perceive our relationship. But this isn't just a distortion seen in ROCD. In the world of psychology, we call a tendency to assume others are paying more attention to us than they really are the *spotlight effect*. Studies have shown that we grossly overestimate the amount of attention people pay to both our positive and our negative qualities (Gilovich, Medvec, and Savitsky 2000), and that we might not be the most accurate judge of what another person is truly thinking, especially in the absence of real evidence.

What qualifies as real evidence? In the example above, Ada has no reason to trust her intrusive thoughts. Her girlfriend has given no indication that she is going to leave and, on the contrary, has shown that she is highly invested in the relationship. If you look around and see that there's no real evidence to support your brain's claims—no one has actually told you that they hate you, or that they think your relationship is a sham, or that your partner is horribly boring—then you just can't allow your brain to tell you otherwise. You've got to run this distortion, like all the other distortions we've explored, through a filter, one that sifts through your fears and allows for a more nuanced truth to emerge. When you notice yourself mind reading, remind yourself of the truth.

**Response:** "I have absolutely no idea what another person is truly thinking, without real evidence."

## Correcting Cognitive Distortions

If the cognitive distortions just described sound familiar, you are far from alone. Everyone falls into these traps from time to time; it's just that those with high anxiety get stuck more often. And while you may not relate to every distortion, it's likely you will recognize yourself and your thought patterns in at least a few. Often, when we stop and really look at our thoughts, we find the doom-and-gloom messaging of the amygdala inconsistent with the world around us. We find this dramatized and scared version of the world to be exhausting and easily toppled. Although gray-area responses like *I have absolutely no idea what will happen in the future* and *Just because I feel something doesn't make it true* are uncomfortable realities to sit in, they challenge us to hold complexity rather than offer quick solutions. They are almost always the more accurate perspective.

We can correct and balance cognitive distortions when they appear by running them through a filter—one meant to catch overgeneralizations and bring much-needed depth and dimension to our thoughts and feelings—to complicate, in a good way, the way we view our relationships and ourselves. But make no mistake: gray-area thinking isn't intuitive, and it's not that comforting. While the responses in the previous section are clearly more rational and balanced than the original intrusive thought, they won't provide immediate relief. Responding with some version of *I don't know*, rather than spiraling into worst-case scenarios or giving ourselves reassurance, positions us firmly in the unknown, where we are vulnerable and exposed. Your anxiety will do anything to avoid this vulnerability, which is why tolerating it is exactly the right muscle to work as we rebalance our thinking. The better we get at inhabiting this vulnerable space without rushing to escape it, the less anxious we become.

## Cognitive Restructuring

One way to practice this balancing act is to use a CBT tool called *cognitive restructuring,* which is the process of noticing our intrusive thoughts when they appear and correcting them to gray, right there, in the moment. Keeping a thought log is a simple and effective way to do this.

**EXERCISE:** Right now, grab a piece of paper and draw three columns on the page. In the left column, list the intrusive (anxiety-producing) thoughts and feelings you have had about your relationship or partner in the past week. These thoughts could start with "What if..." or they could be statements like in the examples in figure 2.

Next, look at the first thought on your list and identify which cognitive distortion your brain has fallen into: all-or-nothing thinking, catastrophizing, emotional reasoning, should or must statements (perfectionism), comparison, or mind reading. In the middle column, label the cognitive distortion. Then, in the righthand column, write the rational response that correlates to that distortion. To avoid giving yourself reassurance, use figure 2 as a guide: keep your responses short and to the point, like the examples; a quick correction is all you need! Remember, the goal is not to feel better right now, but to tolerate the unknown, realize you can cope with discomfort, and feel better in the long term. Once you've worked through one example, repeat this process for the rest of the thoughts on your list. Don't worry if it's hard to believe the rational responses just yet; believing them isn't the point. Rather, the point is to see how you can do something entirely different when intrusive thoughts and feelings show up. It's to do something corrective rather than spiral down a rabbit hole of endless debate with your anxiety, into an argument you can never win.

# Thought Log

| Intrusive Thought | Cognitive Distortion | Rational Response |
|---|---|---|
| If I have a romantic thought about another person, that means I don't truly love my partner. | All-or-nothing thinking | Just because I have a romantic thought about another person doesn't automatically mean my love for my partner is unreal. |
| My friend didn't comment on the picture we posted to social media. They must think we're a bad match or that I'm settling. | Mind reading | Without real evidence, I have no idea what another person is truly thinking. |
| I feel like I should miss my partner more when they're not around. It must mean that I don't actually have OCD, and I'm just in denial of my true feelings. | Emotional reasoning/ perfectionism | Just because I feel like something is wrong doesn't make it true. Feelings don't = facts. It's also unrealistic to expect that I'll miss them all the time. I don't always have to miss my partner to prove that I love them. |
| If I don't figure out how I feel about my relationship, then I will make the biggest mistake of my life and end up miserable, loveless, and alone. | Catastrophizing | I can't predict what will happen in the future, and no matter what happens, I can choose to cope with the outcome. |

Figure 2: Thought Log

After completing this log, you will have carved out a more helpful way to respond to your ROCD when it tries to pull you into a fight. But you don't have to stop there! Continue logging thoughts and making corrections until gray-area responses become second nature. Some of my clients keep a thought log for one week, while others will keep one for months. If you'd like to keep going with this exercise, you can download a blank thought log at http://www.newharbinger.com/47919. If logging these thoughts on paper is tough, or you worry your partner will find them, practice cognitive restructuring in your phone! Or you can simply note when distortions arise and make a mental correction.

It doesn't matter how you practice, as long as you take a few days to notice your habitual thought patterns and do something you've never done before—give a boring stock response rather than get into a fight with your anxiety. There is no perfect way to do this assignment, and it's okay if you don't catch every single distorted thought. Just do your best to notice patterns and gently offer your brain a different response, filtering out the black and white and resting instead in the gray area.

## Becoming a Conscious Consumer

As you fill out your thought log and begin to balance your thinking, you may notice your anxiety starting to lose steam. You might notice that when you engage less with the intrusive voice in your head and stop arguing an endless list of pros and cons, your anxiety has a lot less to say. Just remember that no tool is meant to eradicate your anxiety entirely. That's not the point. The tools in this book aren't meant to snuff out the fire; they're meant to help us withstand the heat. You'll also want to be careful not to use cognitive restructuring as a crutch, answering every single thought that arises with a response or logging hundreds of thoughts a day to avoid feeling the discomfort they arouse. The goal is to pay less attention to our thoughts, not more.

To avoid this, try the 1:3 ratio for correcting intrusive thoughts. Instead of correcting every single thought you have in a given day, aim to give your brain a correction about one out of every three times you notice a distortion. This way you won't get stuck using your responses as a crutch. As you get better at catching and correcting intrusive thoughts in your head, you can respond even less, noticing a distortion (*Oh look, that's all-or-nothing thinking*) but correcting it only one out of every five times the thought appears. Eventually, you might not need to respond at all! You can simply notice your brain is getting stuck in a distorted pattern and gently redirect your attention. No conversation or correction needed.

After months, years, or even a lifetime spent in argument with our thoughts, this shift in the way we respond (or choose not to respond) can be incredibly freeing. Now you get to decide what thoughts you'll be responding to and which bits of news get your attention. You've put yourself back in the driver's seat. Even after a decade of living with and managing OCD, I still use cognitive restructuring to balance out my own thinking. I still remind myself that *I have no idea what will happen in the future* or that *feelings don't equal facts.* I still go back to this very same strategy after I've been knocked off-balance by my OCD. I haven't solved the nagging questions in my anxious brain, and I don't try to anymore. The change for me is that I know that my mind is prone to falling into these grooves and that these grooves have names and telltale patterns. When I have a big reaction to something and feel a flood of anxiety, I step back, name the distortion that's trapping me, and color correct before deciding how to proceed. I try to be a conscious consumer of my thoughts rather than take everything my brain says at face value.

From this more balanced and nuanced point of view, you are poised to take the next step. While correcting your lens is a pivotal part of your recovery, to truly overcome ROCD, you must be willing to do something uncomfortable; you must learn to coexist with it.

# CHAPTER 5

# Acceptance and Commitment Therapy for ROCD

Congratulations! If you have been logging and restructuring your thoughts the past few days (or are continuing to do so), you have begun to create much-needed space between you and your ROCD. Like a couple who could desperately use some time apart, your overdependence on thoughts and feelings needed a correction, and you are well on your way to the freedom you seek. In passing anxiety through a filter, you might have noticed some precious space open between you and your anxiety, the transformative step Austrian psychiatrist and Holocaust survivor Viktor Frankl described when he said, "Between stimulus and response there is a space. In that space is our power to choose our response. In our response lies our growth and our freedom." Without this space, you remain merged with your anxiety and unable to step back to see it for what it is: a projection of fear and the nagging voice of a misfiring amygdala. Like an adult who finally challenges their overprotective parent, you can hear anxiety imploring you to take a sweater when you leave the house (*You'll freeze to death!*) and ultimately decide for yourself if you want to listen.

Cognitive restructuring is a critical foundation in the treatment of ROCD and a cornerstone of my plan with every client who walks through the door. On its own, however, restructuring your thoughts isn't enough. Fending off each and every intrusive thought or feeling with a correction isn't the ultimate answer, because it will keep you in conversation with your anxiety. How do you stop that conversation? You can't. You can only control your response, your half of the dialogue. And while doing this will quiet down the argument, it won't stop your brain from nagging at you to pay attention. If you are to overcome anxiety, you must learn to tolerate it, to coexist with it, rather than attempt to shut down the conversation altogether. Whatever noise is leftover, after you restructure your thoughts and stop arguing pros and cons with your ROCD, must be willingly tolerated and accepted without any intention of changing it.

Willingly tolerating your ROCD may sound like a tall order, but it's absolutely doable. What's more, this practice is the closest thing we have to an answer when it comes to the treatment of anxiety disorders. Thankfully, we don't need to invent the playbook: there's an entire school of therapy that explores the practice of letting thoughts, emotions, and unwanted sensations simply exist while we go on with our lives. It's called acceptance and commitment therapy, and in this chapter, you'll learn to use ACT to think about the kind of person you'd like to be and the kind of relationship you'd like to have, not the one ROCD limits you to. You'll discover that living a fulfilling and meaningful life doesn't require getting rid of ROCD or solving all the burning questions in your mind; it just requires learning to stop paying so much attention to them. Like a fading cinema star, your anxiety still craves your attention and focus. But by willingly tolerating its doom-and-gloom messaging and focusing elsewhere, you activate one of the most effective tools in your arsenal: you make it irrelevant.

## What Is ACT?

Developed by psychologist and researcher Steven Hayes in 1982 as a blend of cognitive and behavioral approaches, acceptance and commitment therapy takes a less confrontational approach to the treatment of unwanted thoughts, feelings, and experiences. When this therapy is used for ROCD, the fundamental goal is to shift your relationship with doubt and intrusive worry from one of antagonism and resistance to one of peaceful coexistence. Rather than trying to eliminate your anxiety, you learn to make friends with it. Why, you might ask, would you want to get chummy with your anxiety? The short answer is, because it's the best way to keep it from running your life. Remember that anxiety in and of itself is not a bad thing; it is a necessary and adaptive threat response, fundamental to our survival. So no matter how hard you try, even if you are a master at catching cognitive traps and restructuring them, the experience of hypervigilance cannot be completely eliminated; your brain has been wired to be on alert. If you can't beat it entirely, you might as well learn to coexist with it.

Learning to coexist with anxiety is all about making space. It's about expanding your tolerance to include things you don't want to feel but have to feel anyway. Imagine you lived in a small one-bedroom apartment in the city with a roommate who drove you crazy but whom you had to live with. Perhaps the roommate left dirty dishes everywhere, was too loud, or followed you around the apartment nagging you to spend more time together. There is no escaping this roommate, and living in cramped quarters means you would feel their presence at every turn. Now imagine that you lived with this same roommate but you hit the lottery and moved into a six-bedroom mansion in the suburbs with a porch and spacious backyard. Yes, the roommate would still be there and would still annoy and frustrate you, but the expansion of space around that annoying roommate would naturally result in less distress. You would feel the presence of your roommate far less than the days when you lived in that tiny one-bedroom apartment.

The thing is, your annoying roommate is here to stay. You can't kick anxiety out of the brain, but you can expand your tolerance and acceptance of it. You can expand your definition of what you're willing to experience and how much you're willing to feel and, by doing so, might not notice this particular roommate quite so much.

You may wonder if you could ever truly be happy with an annoying roommate, no matter how big the space you co-occupied. But ACT therapy isn't all that concerned with achieving happiness, at least not in any traditional sense of the word. In terms of ROCD, we tend to think of complete and consistent happiness as the goal of romantic relationships, but what if this is an unrealistic expectation? What if expecting this kind of happiness is actually making you quite sad?

## Redefining Happiness

All your life, you have learned that pain and discomfort must be solved. You grew up in a world that told you to "suck it up" and "just think positively" rather than cope with the complexity of what it means to be a full-fledged human being in a chaotic world. What very few people will ever tell you is that there is nothing wrong at all with feeling discomfort, sadness, anxiety, or doubt. There is nothing wrong with feeling disconnected from your partner, irritable in your relationship, bored, or turned off. There is nothing wrong with having off-days and depressed days and days when all you want to do is bury your head in the sand and call it quits. Anxiety disorder aside, every single couple you know has significant incompatibilities. In fact, research has shown that 69 percent of all relational problems in a marriage are considered perpetual problems, which means they result from fundamental personality differences between partners, and are never solved, only managed (Gottman and Silver 1999). Imagine how much unnecessary anxiety we create when we live under the impression that our relationships should feel amazing all the time and that perfect happiness is an attainable goal!

The impression that our lives and relationships can and should feel amazing all the time is like MOTO: it's a myth, and a damaging one at that. It perpetuates the false notion that when intrusive thoughts or relationship doubts arise, we have to fight and solve them or else we can't feel okay. But this just isn't true. You can choose to stop fighting and learn to peacefully coexist with intrusive thoughts and feelings and, by doing so, redefine what it means to be happy. Maybe happiness is not the perfect relationship, or a brain free of doubt and anxiety, but rather a reflection of our willingness to accept that which we cannot change and to live life to the fullest anyway. (Again, this is not a call to accept and ignore truly toxic behavior in your partnership, and if you are in an emotionally, physically, or spiritually abusive relationship, then you should not use ACT principles to accept that dysfunction. Making space for relationship anxiety is the goal only if you are in a fundamentally loving and safe relationship.) What we're talking about here is a call to consider the possibility of having a wonderful relationship *and* doubts at the same time: not a solution to eliminate discomfort and anxiety, but a journey to learn how to *feel better by feeling more.*

After all, there is nothing wrong with pain; it is an unavoidable part of being alive. It's really our need to eradicate pain that causes the bulk of our suffering in the short time we have on this Earth.

## Pain vs. Suffering

Pain is inevitable, and although we often try to mask and mitigate its presence by overworking, overthinking, and overdoing, it remains a stubborn truth of the human experience. There is pain in the grief of unmet expectations, in the death of loved ones, and in our own inevitable loss of health. There is pain in having a sensitive amygdala and living with hundreds of intrusive thoughts and feelings every day. There is pain in daily moments of missed connection and misunderstanding between you and those you love. Pain is especially present when you realize your partner can't complete you, that they can't solve all your problems and take away your fears: it was never their job to do so. "Life is pain, Highness," the character of Westley tells the princess in the beloved classic *The Princess Bride.* "Anyone who says differently is selling something."

But while pain is unavoidable in life and in love, suffering is optional. Suffering is our resistance to, judgment of, and attempt to eradicate the natural pain of living. It's the story we tell ourselves about what feelings or experiences we can and can't tolerate. Imagine you're at a wedding with your partner, and your ROCD begins to act up, sending you messages like *You aren't as happy as they are. They're so in love! You didn't feel this way on your wedding day.* All you wanted was to enjoy the wedding, and now you are caught in a spiral of comparison and catastrophizing. Your anxiety skyrockets, and you leave the party anxious about your relationship and depressed that your day was ruined because of ROCD. Here's the thing: you can't control the fact that your brain was triggered by attending the wedding; this is pain, and it is unavoidable. But where you will experience the most discomfort isn't actually in the pain: it's in your *resistance* to the pain; it's in the suffering. Like that finger trap toy we talked about in chapter 1, you don't suffer because you have intrusive thoughts; you suffer because of your attempts to escape, control, and disprove them. Believe it or not, you can feel triggered at the wedding, notice intrusive thoughts and anxiety, and *choose to do nothing* about them, allowing them to pass through your mind like grains of sand through a sieve.

Struggling against pain can look like this:

- Judging (*I'm such a horrible person for having these thoughts.*)

- Resisting (*I don't want to be thinking these things, least of all today! I refuse to feel bad on what should be a happy occasion.*)

- Hating (*I hate that I have to deal with anxiety. It's ruining my life.*)

- Thought stopping (*No, brain! Stop having these thoughts!*)

- Bracing against (tightening and stiffening of muscles)

We suffer precisely because we believe we shouldn't be feeling pain in the first place. *I shouldn't have to deal with ROCD,* we think, or *Relationships are supposed to be easy and fulfilling, why am I so anxious?* We want to be happy, in the classic sense of the word, and we believe the only way to do so is by eliminating and solving the nagging questions in our mind, even though doing this hasn't worked. So far, it hasn't given us the answer or certainty we seek. So why do we do it then? Why do we struggle against pain and anxiety if it's so unhelpful? Because we are wired to! And because our instinct to fight, avoid, and resist pain is actually quite natural. Humans evolved in an environment in which most of the pain of living was external and could be solved using three strategies: fight, flight, or freeze. We evolved to run from famine and drought, fight possible attackers, and avoid situations that could hurt us.

This strategy worked for our ancestors, and it still works fine when the threat is external. But what if the assault is in your mind rather than in the bushes outside your camp? What should you do if you can't just run from anxiety, attack it, or avoid it, hoping it will go away and leave you alone? You can use that wonderfully evolved brain of yours to do something miraculous; you can choose to stop being reactive, lay down your weapons, and willingly accept that which you cannot control.

When you stop struggling, you stop suffering.

## Making Peace with Anxiety

Your anxiety loves a good fight, like a game of tug-of-war with your mind. And because of our wiring, we believe that if we keep pulling and resisting against our anxiety, eventually we'll win. But what would happen if you let go of the other side of the rope? What would it be like if you stopped fighting mental messages of doom and, instead, allowed those messages to exist unexplored? I know it seems dangerous or even irresponsible; not addressing pain goes directly against human instinct. But in the treatment of ROCD, adopting a stance of nonresistance is absolutely key to recovery; I have yet to see one person truly recover without acceptance as part of their strategy.

As long as we believe something shouldn't exist—whether it be traffic on the way to an important meeting or intrusive thoughts and doubt—our mind will continue to produce warning messages and heightened anxiety whenever that experience arises. And while you can't change the fact that you have anxiety or ROCD anymore than you can wish away traffic, you can change your definition of what is bad or intolerable. It all starts with acceptance, with letting the thoughts and feelings you have (*He's not the one! I don't have all the right feelings! I should be more certain!*) simply be there, without resisting them, exploring them, or fixing them one bit.

## Practicing Acceptance

I know it can be overwhelming to think about what acceptance really means, let alone practice it. The concept can seem so esoteric and out there, and you may think, *Okay, this sounds great. I'd love to find a way to live peacefully with my pain and all that. But how do I actually practice acceptance?* This chapter will give you an arsenal of strategies to accept unwanted thoughts, feelings, and experiences, and I promise you don't need to be an experienced yogi or a monk for them to work. But first, I want to dispel some of the common myths I hear every single day about what it means to practice acceptance, the kinds of misconceptions that can hijack this portion of your recovery if you believe them. You may think that asking you to accept your ROCD sounds like I'm asking you to accept defeat, but acceptance is really the mature realization that fighting was never the answer.

Here are some common misconceptions about acceptance:

**"If I accept my thoughts, I will make them worse."** This won't happen, though you may at first experience more thoughts when you loosen the reins on your anxiety. Like heavy drinking at the end 1920s Prohibition, your anxiety might have a short phase of rebellion as you loosen your grip! It's realistic to expect a bit of a spike after months or years of labeling certain things as forbidden, bad, or dirty. But if you hold the course, you will find that this spike is only temporary. Your anxiety will realize you're no longer fighting off what it warns you about, and it will eventually lose steam. The tricky part is hanging in and trusting you'll get there, even as your anxiety does everything it can to regain your attention.

**"Accepting my thoughts means that I agree with them."** Accepting something is not the same as agreeing with or liking it. Accepting it just means you realize the futility of fighting. Acceptance does not ask that you agree with the content of your ROCD thoughts or feelings; it simply asks that you be willing to make space for them. And, contrary to *manifestation,* which is the concept of concentrating on what you want by thinking about it and funneling your energy toward it, acceptance is a surrendering that says, *Anxiety, you can be here or not; it doesn't make much difference to me.* After all, you can allow someone with whom you disagree to sit at your table without needing to prove them wrong or engaging with them, right? Couldn't you do the same thing with ROCD?

**"Acceptance is too hard. I don't have the discipline to make it work."** Yes, practicing acceptance is hard and requires intentional effort. But which is harder, learning to allow that which you cannot change or spending your entire life fighting and struggling against anxiety? Accepting unwanted experiences is counterintuitive, and most of us are out of practice, so expect this part to be difficult at first. Your brain will probably fight back, sending messages that the difficulty of changing your behavior is a sign that you shouldn't be practicing acceptance in the first place. Like the first few repetitions of a new dance routine or exercise at the gym, you will be unsure and might doubt your ability to push through. You'll feel ungainly and worry you're doing it all wrong, messing it up! But if you hold steady and tolerate the awkwardness of this new approach, you'll get the hang of it. You'll come to see that resistance to anxiety is exhausting and fruitless, and acceptance is a much more sustainable strategy in the lifelong management of ROCD.

**"What if I accept my thoughts and realize what they say is true?"** If you truly have ROCD, this outcome is unlikely. Generally, people who seek treatment for ROCD—and, for that matter, anyone fighting this hard to stay in a relationship —are probably into their partner. That being said, if not resisting your thoughts does allow a deep truth to arise, you can honor it and then decide what to do with it. I know it's triggering to risk an outcome you don't want—that your truth could be an ultimate decision to leave your partnership—but if you only do the work in this book to avoid reaching that outcome, you will have been engaging in a grand compulsion. Growth in life is directly correlated to our willingness to take risks, and while it's unlikely that you'll realize you truly don't love your partner, or that you're in the wrong relationship, you must be willing to tolerate that small possibility if you hope to get to the other side of ROCD.

## Your Acceptance Arsenal

Now that we've addressed some common concerns, it's time to begin developing your acceptance arsenal, the practical tools you'll need to loosen your anxiety's grip and, thus, release the struggle. First up is a tool called *naming the thought*, which is all about helping yourself see your thoughts and feelings for exactly what they are, rather than for the all-powerful truth your anxiety presents them as.

### Naming the Thought

Take a moment to follow along with this short exercise. Close your eyes and think the most distressing thought to you at this moment. Maybe it's *I'm in denial, and I'm really not in love with my partner* or perhaps it's *What if I don't make the right decision, and I live a life full of regret,* or even *I'm a monster for having these kinds of thoughts.* Whatever the thought of the day is, say it to yourself and notice how it makes you feel. Do you notice a tightness in your chest or a slight scrunching of your eyebrows? Do you notice a feeling of discomfort or anxiety in your chest as you repeat the thought to yourself? Perhaps you notice a rush in your gut or a slight pang of pain. When you repeat your fears to yourselves in this direct, factual manner (*I'm in denial* or *I'm a monster*), your brain registers the thought as fact and instantly triggers a threat response: anxiety. This is an example of an ACT concept called *thought fusion,* where we become so stuck in our thoughts that we can't see them for what they truly are, just mental noise. We can't find the separation necessary to stay objective when thoughts arise, and thus we find it difficult to modulate our reaction to them.

Now try the exercise again, but this time make a small tweak. Tell yourself, instead, *I'm having the thought that I'm in denial* or *I'm having the feeling that I'm a monster.* Notice if there is a shift in your body, perhaps a slight loosening of your muscles or a relaxation in your breathing. You might notice that the thought just isn't as sticky! By simply labeling thoughts or feelings for what they are, we begin to separate ourselves from their content and view them from an observational (objective) stance; we become less stuck. If you want to play this game at an expert level, try saying *I'm noticing that I'm having the thought that I'm a monster/ in denial/ destined for a life of regret.* At this level you're playing a meta-naming game with your anxiety, recognizing not only the thought but also the objective observer inside you noticing the thought as it's happening.

If fusion describes a lack of healthy distance and objectivity between our thoughts and feelings, then our goal is to carve out some space to *defuse* from ROCD thinking. How does defusion relate to acceptance, and how can it help you better manage ROCD? Think about how you felt in the first part of the exercise when you were firmly fused with your thoughts. My guess is that when the distressing thought presented as a fact (*You're in denial! You're a monster!*), it was hard not to resist and struggle against the thought's presence in your mind. It probably felt quite difficult to imagine just letting the thought exist, unexplored or unsolved. But when you named that mental statement as a thought or a feeling, you took away its power. Defusion addresses the tight knot of our thinking and pulls it apart, allowing us to see painful emotions and thoughts for what they really are, just thoughts or feelings and not neces-sarily the truth. From a healthy distance, you can then choose not to pay much attention to them at all! You can simply let them be.

Go ahead and store this naming-the-thought tool in your mental toolbox along with the cognitive restructuring you learned in the last chapter. Next up is tool aimed at increasing acceptance, decreasing suffering, and, thus, alleviating your anxiety. It's time to meet the bully in your brain and learn to lean in.

## Leaning In

*Leaning into* discomfort is an ACT tool that will help you tolerate ROCD. It's acknowledging that ROCD acts like a bully and that the best way to manage a bully may at times feel incredibly counterintuitive.

To illustrate how leaning in works, take yourself back to when you were in middle school, a time rife with insecurity and the pressure to fit in, and recall what the It item of clothing was at that time. Say it was a pair of expensive shoes, and let's say you happened to convince your parents to buy you these shoes. Now imagine yourself walking confidently in on the first day of school. *Nothing can get me down!* you think. *This is going to be my year!* But just then, the school bully (let's call her Jenny) waltzes up. She takes one look at your shoes, looks back up at you, and snarks, "Oh, so you think you're cool now? You might have the shoes, but you're still a huge loser, and no one will ever like you." Ouch. That really hurts. My guess is that your amygdala would register this threat and prompt one of its go-to strategies: fight, flight, or freeze. You might exhibit aggression (fight). Maybe you would run away from Jenny (flight) or, if nothing else, stand there shocked and silent, not knowing how to respond and fearing anything you say could bring on more of an assault (freeze). Any of these responses would make sense, but one thing is certain. If you reacted in one of these ways, Jenny would be back tomorrow, ready to torment you and watch you struggle all over again.

The thing is, bullies love a reaction. They love riling you up, and they live off your negative attention. Like Jenny, ROCD is a mental bully, pulling out just the right trigger (*Why did you notice that attractive person walking by? How can this be real if you have so many negative thoughts?*) to get you going and catch your attention. Remember, OCD doesn't attach to just anything; it recognizes what matters most to you and goes for that. So with ROCD, your OCD latches onto your desire to be in a good relationship, and because this matters so much to you, you'll fight even harder to prove or disprove what ROCD says. You'll get caught up in its trap. Okay, so the bully knows how to get you where it hurts, but how about the bully? What is ROCD's Achilles' heel?

The answer is irrelevance. The best way to defeat a bully is to ignore what they say or do, and the same is true for ROCD. Now imagine that we repeat the story but with a twist. You show up with the slick new pair of shoes on the first day of school, and Jenny looks over and says, "Here comes that loser thinking she's so cool with her new shoes!" But this time, you respond differently: "Jenny, hey! Thank you so much for saying so. You know, I agree with you. I am a massive loser. It's amazing I even manage to put together an outfit in the morning with how much of a loser I am! You seem to know me so well, so maybe we could become best friends and spend every single day together? What do you think?"

Jenny is going to have a vastly different reaction to this kind of feedback. Instead of arguing with her, crying, or running away, you chose to thank her? Instead of giving her what she wanted, you subverted her expectations and took the power right out of her words! Of course, what she said was still hurtful; no one wants to be called names or told they aren't likeable. But when you respond to bullies, including the one in your mind, with an attitude of playful indifference, you win by losing or, rather, you win by not engaging at all.

You might tell your bullying thoughts, *Thanks, brain. Maybe I am with the ugliest/stupidest/least interesting person in the world. Maybe I am in denial, and my life will be ruined because I chose not to listen to my truth. Oh well!* If you don't fight your thoughts, there is no struggle. There isn't anyone pulling on the other end of the tug-of-war rope. Your anxiety won't have anything to feed off of and will grow bored, the same way that Jenny the bully would. Remember, acceptance doesn't mean you have to agree deep down. And you probably don't actually think that your partner is the ugliest, stupidest, or least compatible person for you in the world, just like you wouldn't really want to be Jenny's best friend. But by leaning into discomfort, you drop your end of the tug-of-war rope. You instantly remove the fight between you and your ROCD.

**EXERCISE:** Use this strategy the next time you experience an ROCD thought: respond by exaggeratedly leaning into the worst-case message it sends you. It helps to imagine yourself responding to the bully in your brain with a blasé, indifferent tone when using this tool (if you can't make it funny or lighthearted, this might not be the strategy for you). I recommend using a physical shrug and a solid dose of sarcasm when using leaning in. Have a little fun with it!

Here are a few examples of how to lean into ROCD.

**ROCD says:** "I'm not sure you're in the right relationship, because you don't have those in-love feelings."

**Lean-in response:** "Wow, thanks for that heads-up, brain! You know what? I'm almost positive I've chosen wrong, and I'm just duping myself because I was bored and wanted to ruin my life. I couldn't be any less into my partner. Guess I messed up!"

**ROCD says:** "Are you sure he loves you enough? He's been acting off lately, and you are a lot to handle sometimes."

**Lean-in response:** "Brain, you are so talented at bringing the truth to my attention. I bet he's been stringing me along all this time because he's sadistic, and I'm just part of an elaborate game. Glad you warned me!"

**ROCD says:** "You don't feel like having sex tonight. There isn't enough physical chemistry, and you're better off as friends!

**Lean-in response:** "Yup brain! That sounds about right. We have zero physical chemistry. In fact, I can barely stand to be next to my wife most days. We have some fun plans I don't want to miss this weekend, but maybe Monday would be a good time to file for divorce? What do you think?"

Are you laughing a little? Good. Leaning in helps you accept and expand because it reveals the silliness behind anxiety's doomsday story, like when Dorothy meets the actual Oz and finds a small, scared man rather than the imposing villain everyone is terrified of. After a good chuckle, your anxiety is suddenly much easier to tolerate. With anxiety defanged, you can turn your attention elsewhere, in a direction that's much more fulfilling and meaningful. Responding to your intrusive thoughts in this way will likely feel dangerous and exhilarating; you've never dared speak to the bully in quite this way before! Your mental bully might double down with a response like *Oh, so you are okay with what I'm saying. See, I told you this relationship was all a lie!* But this too is just another thought you can lean into, shrugging your shoulders and playing cool, until the bully grows bored of your inattention and loosens its grip. When you stop treating thoughts as inherently meaningful, important, or good or bad, you dilute their power over you. You can then choose to pay attention to them or not, depending on what you decide is most helpful for your life.

## Promoting Your Values

Yet another tool that you can use to decrease struggle and increase acceptance is to categorize your thoughts not as good or bad, as we often do, but as either helpful or unhelpful. Remember that your brain is hard-wired to protect you and remind you of potential danger, so if you label a thought as bad, you sensitize your brain to that thought, telling it *There could be danger here, so stay on alert!* The last thing you want is to keep your brain on alert, or give it any good reason to keep looking for danger. A better solution is to drop the judgment over whether something you're experiencing is good or bad, to simply ask, *Does paying attention to this thought, feeling, or worry serve me? Does it align with and promote my values as a person and partner, or does paying attention to this take me further away from the kind of life and relationship I desire?*

To answer this question and hone in on which thoughts and behaviors are helpful, you've got to know your own personal values. Identifying your values will help you see what kind of partner you want to be and what sort of relationship you ultimately want to have. One size doesn't fit all, and values are different for every single person. The wonderful thing is, that once you know your values, you will no longer have to ask if each and every thought, feeling, or worry is meaningful or true, or spend hours analyzing their origin. You can simply ask yourself, *Is it helpful?* If not, there's no need for further discussion. You can let it be, and go on. You can decide what messages deserve attention, which thoughts and feelings align with your values. If something doesn't match up, you can move right past it! You decide what's unhelpful or unhelpful, what's worthy or unworthy of your time and attention.

But first you will need to explore your values.

**EXERCISE:** Start by imagining the ideal (but still realistic) relationship, and then answer the following questions. Even better, write down your responses for future review:

- If you had no anxiety or fear clouding you, what kind of partner would you want to be? What things would you be doing differently?

- If your partner were to describe you ten years in the future and what you bring to the relationship, what would you want them to say about you? How would you want them to describe the way you made them feel?

- Ideally, how would you want others to describe your partnership if they were on the outside looking in? What kind of partnership would you want to represent?

- Use three adjectives to describe the quality of your ideal partnership, such as adventurous, joyful, loving, passionate, explorative, or intellectual.

The answers to these questions reveal something very important. They reveal your values and, beyond that, your motivation for doing this work. The life, love story, and partnership you described is what makes tolerating uncertainty worth it; it's what powers your growth. Maybe you look at your answers and recognize that listening to fear and anxiety hasn't gotten you where you're looking to go, that it's time for a different approach.

## VALUES VS. GOALS

The ACT concept of values is often confused with the concept of goals, but values and goals are fundamentally different. Values are continuous guides to living and do not have one definite endpoint, unlike the goal of running a marathon or of owning a home. Values (like kindness, growth, or acceptance) are directional; they orient our choices and inform why we do what we do and where we are headed in life. Living with a sensitive amygdala makes knowing our values even more imperative because while thoughts and feelings may come and go like weather in the anxious mind, our values remain stable. They are a trustworthy guide through the storm of intrusive doubt.

The thing is, you don't need to feel good to act in line with your values. That's the beauty of it. You don't need to feel love to act out of love; you don't need to feel 100 percent committed for you to commit. ACT expert Russ Harris says, "The feeling of love comes and goes on a whim; you can't control it. But the action of love is something you can do, regardless of how you are feeling" (2009, 9). With that principle in mind, we can see that helpful actions are those that keep us in alignment with our values, regardless of how we are feeling in the moment, while unhelpful behaviors are those that take us out of alignment and away from the life and the partnership we've always wanted. When we make choices based on what anxiety wants, we get tossed around by our mood and preferences, which shift throughout the day, sometimes even from one hour to the next. No, we need something more solid to hang our hat on; we need to drop deeper into our core values.

Amir's story shows what values look like in action:

*Amir is a father of two young children, who came to treatment looking to work through ROCD symptoms that had gotten worse after the birth of his second child and now threatened his marriage.*

*Lately, he had grown cold toward his wife and reported feeling like he couldn't get close because his anxious thoughts were "just too loud." When we explored his values, Amir said he'd always hoped to be in a relationship that was adventurous and spontaneous, and he imagined traveling the world together as a family when the boys were a little older. He hoped to be the kind of husband who made his wife feel wanted, appreciated, and supported and that they could be good parents as well as passionate partners who spent time helping one another grow personally and spiritually. Amir valued novelty, a close and loving partnership, as well as a spiritual connection with the person he loved.*

*Once his values were identified, Amir could stop judging his compulsions and ROCD behaviors as good or bad and start seeing them as simply helpful or unhelpful in the context of the values he wanted to embody in his relationship. I asked him to reflect on his recent compulsion, an act of avoidance in which he isolated himself from his wife after a particularly difficult day of thoughts. Avoidance felt good in the moment, but was it ultimately helpful? Did avoiding his wife after he was triggered make him more of the loving, connected partner he wanted to be? Did that behavior increase the passion in his relationship, or did avoidance take him in the opposite direction? Amir realized that by giving into his compulsion he had stepped further away from the kind of partner he wanted to be; giving into avoidance was unhelpful to his ultimate vision of love and life.*

Had Amir done the difficult task of tolerating his anxiety spike and chosen to engage with his wife rather than avoid her, he would have done something difficult but helpful. In tolerating discomfort, he would be more in alignment with his values in the relationship and would probably feel better in the long run.

This isn't to say that all your thoughts and actions should be helpful all the time. That's way too much pressure. One unhelpful choice in a sea of helpful ones will not permanently misalign you, and you can always find your way back to your values if you go astray. But it can be useful to remember what you're working for, especially on the tough days, on the days when your anxiety is spiking and all you want to do is run and hide. Are you working toward better intimacy, toward increased closeness and vulnerability? Do you want to be the kind of partner who laughs and lets loose? The person who has anxiety but doesn't let it control their life? Determine your values, and then orient yourself in their direction, regardless of what you think or how you feel in the moment.

## Paying Attention to Physical Cues

In this chapter, we've looked at how mental struggle and resistance put you at odds with ROCD and increase your suffering, and how fighting, hating, and arguing with anxiety only makes things worse. But there remains one sneaky form of resistance yet to be mentioned. This resistance is frequently overlooked and involves not your mind but your body. Believe it or not, it's just as important to recognize and release physical resistance as it is to let go of mental resistance. To see what I mean, try the following experiment.

**EXERCISE:** Take a moment to consider the most triggering quality about your partner or partnership. Maybe it's a physical feature you dislike or some perceived flaw in the quality of your love or connection. How does thinking about this trigger make you feel? Pay attention to what's happening in your body right now. Do you feel an increase in tension? Do you notice a feeling of tightness in your breath or a collapsing of your posture?

Often when doing this exercise with clients, I notice their shoulders begin to creep up to their ears. I notice their breath go shallow and rapid and watch their forehead scrunch up as they close in on themselves right in front of me. These are all signs of physical resistance, a bodily struggle against something unwanted, a struggle that is no less damaging than any other compulsion discussed in this book. Like all forms of struggle, bracing your body against the invisible ROCD enemy sends a message of threat to your amygdala that something is wrong, intolerable, and bad. There's no real threat, but your brain doesn't get the message, because your body is responding as if you were in imminent danger.

This is one reason why breath work and meditation are hugely important to anxiety management: if you relax your body when triggered, you send the all-good message to your amygdala. The same way that levity interrupted the spiral in the story of the bully, you can interrupt anxiety by releasing physical tension as you notice it build in your body. By engaging in an opposing action, like breathing slowly when you feel short of breath or opening up your posture when you feel like scrunching in on yourself, you prove a powerful point. You show yourself and your anxiety that you are safe and have what it takes to cope, no matter how scary your thoughts or feelings may be.

## Taking Stock of Your Anxiety Toolbox

Before moving on, let's take a moment to review what's in your toolbox so far. In chapter 4, you learned how to recognize the cognitive tricks the ROCD brain plays and to use restructuring to gently challenge and correct these distorted patterns of thinking. Hopefully, this foundation has allowed you to begin separating from your intrusive thoughts and feelings, as it shows you that not everything your brain says is true or meaningful, and not everything you think is automatically factual.

In this chapter, we pivoted to ACT, which helps you with the anxious noise that even your best efforts to restructure can leave behind. You learned to create a healthier relationship to unwanted experiences by reducing struggle and resistance and by increasing acceptance. You practiced defusion through naming your thoughts and practiced leaning in when ROCD tries to pick a fight. Finally, you explored your value system and the deeper reason for this work, which will help you continue to evolve toward a more peaceful relationship to life's inevitable pain.

How and when do you use these tools? The choice is largely personal, and there is no right way to do so. You may be attracted to cognitive restructuring and want to concentrate on this first, perhaps recognizing *I'm catastrophizing right now and can't predict the future,* and then follow this thought with the leaning-in strategy, *But you know what brain, maybe you're right, and my marriage is absolutely destined for the gutter. Oh well!* Other times you might simply notice that a thought is unhelpful and choose to mentally walk on by. As you experiment with these tools, you will realize which ones suit you best, and you'll devise your own special cocktail of strategies for ROCD management. A note of caution: no strategy or tool taught in this book is meant to eradicate anxiety altogether, and it's wise not to make "feeling good" the goal. Likewise, don't beat yourself up if the tools don't work instantly. Remember that by making space for things that we don't want to feel, think, or experience, we cease to feel, think, or experience them so much. We also increase our ability and willingness to tolerate them; we increase our mental real estate.

The beauty of ACT for ROCD is that nothing needs to change for you to decide, right now, that you will stop fighting a war you were never meant to win. So from here on out, notice when you're struggling against your anxiety and commit to dropping your weapons. Notice judgment around having ROCD (*I'm such a horrible partner; how could I think these things?*) and let that judgment go. If you notice your body tightening or breath shortening when you listen to a friend talk about finding The One, relax your body: let the discomfort be without stiffening against it. If you have one of those days when you are railing against God and the heavens for giving you OCD, and you feel at the end of your rope, take a deep breath and be with the pain rather than hate it. The moment you decide a feeling or experience shouldn't exist is the very moment that feeling gains power over you, so make anxiety an acceptable experience. If you are willing to take the risk of full-heartedly allowing discomfort a seat at your table, without wishing it away, you might find that something spectacular happens. When you stop fighting, hating, and resisting it, ROCD often chooses to walk away, all on its own.

# CHAPTER 6

# Exposure Therapy for ROCD

I can remember the day I walked into my first session with an OCD specialist, a skilled clinician whom I credit with helping me through some of my toughest days early on in my diagnosis. By then, in my early twenties, I had already spent years in traditional talk therapy, which had helped me process my childhood but had never quite addressed the spinning and incessant quality of my OCD. I remember thinking *What could this person do for me that I haven't already tried myself? How could this treatment approach really make much of a difference when I've spent so many hours talking about my anxiety without significantly moving the needle?* I had spent so much time thinking, talking, and journaling about anxiety without much progress. But I was about to realize what I had been missing, that the major component of recovery from anxiety was not in processing how I felt, but in taking action to change it. I was about to face my fears head-on through a technique called exposure and response prevention. In this chapter, I'll teach you to do the same.

So far, we've explored how ROCD develops through a combination of nature, nurture, and our fascination with MOTO, the perfect love story at the core of our unrealistic expectations of love and partnership. You've learned about the common cognitive traps in ROCD and how to spring those traps using cognitive restructuring from the world of CBT. Finally, chapter 5 helped you befriend the bully in your brain with playful nonchalance and nonresistance, using skills from ACT.

It's time to put this knowledge and training to use, taking a leap of faith straight into the heart of what you've been avoiding the most. Perhaps you'll expose yourself to the frightening possibility that the person you love will leave you or that you'll never have the kind of passion or connection you dreamed of. Maybe you'll face the worry that you've made the wrong decision or that, in choosing your partner, you've forsaken a better match, someone with whom you wouldn't have doubts. No matter what shape your fear takes, the only way to recover from ROCD is to feel the deep vulnerability at its core and learn that you can tolerate it; to feel experientially, rather than just intellectually, that you really can cope, that you'll be okay. Exposure and response prevention allows you to face your fears therapeutically, and it is the most powerful agent of change in overcoming anxiety disorders.

## What Is Exposure Therapy?

ERP is a therapeutic technique that involves exposure to a feared scenario, to intentionally trigger and raise anxiety levels, followed by response prevention, which is the elimination of any kind of behavior meant to neutralize that anxiety spike. So how does this work with ROCD? As an example, imagine I were to ask you to spend time with an attractive colleague who triggers the fear *What if I'm actually in love with my colleague and end up cheating on my spouse?* Naturally, asking you to spend time with anyone whom you've been avoiding for months would cause a spike in your anxiety and discomfort. Response prevention describes the corrective actions you would take before, during, and after interacting with your colleague so that you would not give into any compulsions. That is, instead of checking your attraction to the colleague or confessing your intrusive thoughts to your partner as soon as you got home, you would tolerate the anxiety you feel without responding in any way. ERP asks that you just ride the wave of anxiety up and inevitably back down again. If you were doing this exposure, I would ask you to repeat it for a number of days or weeks until you realized that you can tolerate the pain without needing to escape through compulsive behavior, and realized that the scary outcome your brain is sure will come true (cheating on your partner) isn't all that likely to occur.

Sounds nice in theory, right? Face your fears and you'll get better. But you may worry about actually being able to tolerate that anxiety when it shows up, to experience discomfort without trying to escape, solve, or get rid of it. It's hard to cut compulsions when you've been triggered, when fear hijacks your thoughts and feelings and barrages you with doubt. But you're not heading into the heart of fear alone, and while meeting your fears head-on may seem like scaling an impossibly steep mountain, you've got the tools! You've spent the last two chapters gaining valuable strategies for coping, the kind that take the bite out of anxiety's message and empower you to tolerate uncertainty. You are well equipped for the challenge ahead.

The power of ERP lies less in the exposure (E) and more in what comes after we face our fear, the response prevention (RP): the willingness to stand your ground as anxiety hurls its most compelling doubts and worries your way.

## Learning to Let Anxiety Be

We tend to believe that unless we take it upon ourselves to escape discomfort, it will go on and on forever, endlessly torturing us. But even your biggest spike will naturally resolve if you *just leave it alone.* Harvard neuroscientist Jill Bolte-Taylor (2009) found that the average life span of an emotion, if we can allow it to exist without any resistance whatsoever, is only about ninety seconds. She calls this the ninety-second rule, and it applies to all painful emotional spikes, including your anxiety. Not responding to a blaring warning signal that proclaims your biggest fears is a hard thing to do, even for ninety seconds. But remember, there is a big difference between true threat and an ROCD false alarm. If we can recognize when anxiety is behind the microphone, we can refuse to engage with the fear propaganda it spews forth and instead act in ways that promote connection and clarity in our relationships. We can choose to act in line with our values and regain the quality of our lives.

Through ERP, anxiety loses credibility. With every repetition of an exposure (every time you do something that you fear, and you survive), with every ninety-second round of emotional intensity you tolerate, your fear becomes less convincing and wields less influence over you. By the fourth or fifth time you repeat an exposure, you've begun to redistribute the balance of power in the relationship between you and ROCD. You've brought fear back down to size. By facing your fears head-on, without reinforcing them through compulsive avoidance, reassurance, or rumination, you desensitize your brain's threat response and prove two important points:

1. The feared outcome most often does not occur, and you can choose to cope if it does.

2. You are strong enough to tolerate anxiety and discomfort, and when you don't try to neutralize it, anxiety will decrease all on its own.

Imagine how powerful it could be to turn toward anxiety and discomfort with a bring-it-on attitude, to kick it out of the driver's seat of your life. As you stop listening so much to what your ROCD wants you to do—to check for optimal connection, to seek reassurance, to find the answer—you'll rewire the need for absolute certainty. You'll slowly but surely open up to vulnerability and learn that you can tolerate it in your relationship. With time and practice, you might come to see that sitting with vulnerability is not just an painful necessity, but a pathway to the exact kind of love and life you've always dreamed of.

## Facing Uncertainty

Before we get started, remember that nothing in this book can protect you from the pain of living with and loving another person. ERP isn't meant to give you certainty that scary things like loss, regret, and divorce won't happen, but it will show you that those scary things are far less likely to occur than your brain says they are. More importantly, facing your fears head-on will prove that, no matter how loud anxiety is or how convincing its messaging, you're stronger than you think. You can handle all the noise and uncertainty ROCD throws your way and still choose to live life exactly the way you want—driven by values, not by fear. Behavioral therapies like ERP are sometimes criticized for addressing surface concerns rather than getting to the core of our suffering, the way more traditional talk therapy approaches do. But done correctly, ERP has the power not only to manage our anxiety, but to heal us to our very core.

Recall from chapter 2 that attachment injuries (trauma in your relationship with primary caregivers) inform and exacerbate the development of ROCD. If you experienced neglect or rejection in childhood or if you had an overly controlling or overly chaotic childhood, it's possible your ROCD developed in part as a psychological defense meant to protect you from experiencing that same pain in your adult relationships. Studies have shown that people with insecure attachment styles (anxious, avoidant, or disorganized attachment) underestimate their ability to cope with distress while simultaneously finding it harder to regulate their emotions when triggered (Doron, et al. 2012), a combination that can shut down the risk-taking necessary to find and maintain meaningful love. Viewing relationships through a lens of potential threat makes it hard to trust and relax, keeping you on edge even if you've found a person completely unlike the caregiver(s) who hurt you.

Though we cannot go back and change our parenting, there is absolutely hope. Attachment theory supports the idea of gaining earned security, of healing our attachment wounds through healthy adult relationships and overriding old programming about what it means to be in connection with another person. One incredible effect of ERP for ROCD is that, by facing your fears every day with an attitude of willingness, you take a profound leap of faith toward healing attachment injuries. You challenge the idea that all relationships lead to disappointment, you challenge the idea that if you were truly to be known, you would be rejected, and you challenge the notion that all relationships involve pain or abandonment. ROCD can make you feel like you're always one foot in and one foot out of your relationship, but you'll never know what a wonderfully healing space your relationship can be if you never actually commit to one wholeheartedly. By jumping in the water with both feet and tolerating the fear that comes with it, you take a profound leap toward healing the wound at the very core of your being. You work to earn the secure attachment you were dénied as a child.

It's true! ERP can be pretty life changing.

## If You Need Help

The ERP guide presented in this chapter is an introduction to this therapeutic technique and how to conduct it on your own. This is hard work. Facing your fears can be incredibly triggering and may bring up previously unexplored anxieties or open the floodgates to pain and grief not yet healed. After all, these are fears that you've probably been avoiding for months, if not years. If you become confused or overwhelmed as you try ERP, consider working with a qualified OCD specialist to coach you through your response to discomfort. Even a few sessions of ERP can have a big impact (see resources at the back of this book).

## Exposure and Response Prevention for ROCD

So grab your tools and let's get started! It's time to begin scaling the mountain. The first step in practicing ERP is to figure out which fears you want to face and in what order. You'll want to both challenge your fears head-on and avoid moving so fast that you become overwhelmed. To help with this, you'll need a map, and in the practice of ERP, this map is called an *exposure hierarchy*. This hierarchy is a list of your feared scenarios organized in increasing order of difficulty.

Like an athlete building muscle, you'll face your fears gently at first, starting with lighter weights and fewer repetitions to build strength and confidence before progressing to the scarier numbers on your hierarchy. The process of slowly building up your tolerance to discomfort is called *graduated* exposure and is an excellent way to ensure you maintain motivation for the long road ahead.

It's completely natural to feel nervous and a little excited about finally having a plan to work with your anxiety, and there's good reason to feel hopeful! ERP is the gold standard of treatment for ROCD and anxiety disorders because it works. Studies have shown that two-thirds of patients who received ERP experienced improvement in OCD symptoms, and approximately one-third were considered to be recovered, which means they no longer qualified for a diagnosis of OCD (Eddy et al. 2004). I've personally seen thousands of people recover and go on to have meaningful and significant relief from ROCD, crediting ERP with their success. But to get the most out of this process, you'll have to start slowly, move steadily, and maintain the attitude of a marathon runner who's in it for the long haul. ERP is as much a therapeutic technique as it is a mindset: a willingness to face your fears, day in and day out, and to some degree for the rest of your life. ERP isn't a onetime fix.

## Creating Your Exposure Hierarchy

The first step in putting together an exposure hierarchy is figuring out what you want it to consist of: which situations, thoughts, and behaviors you most want to target. You will want to think about the compulsions that you are motivated to change, the ones that detract most from the quality of your connection and relationship. You will also want to think about the particular anxiety-producing situations that trigger those compulsions. It's these anxiety-producing situations that will make up your exposure hierarchy (see the example in figure 3).

You may wonder, with the thousands of thoughts running through your head every day, which behaviors should be considered compulsions and which would be considered typical aspects of any relationship? How can you tell the difference, for example, between recreational analysis and unhelpful rumination? What about the difference between asking for support and compulsively seeking reassurance?

## NEED-BASED BEHAVIORS

The key is to ask yourself if your behavior is a *want* or a *need*. In other words, how much flexibility do you feel around changing this thought pattern/avoidance/reassurance/ritual? For example, if you've been thinking about a pleasant interaction with an attractive acquaintance and notice that you don't feel too much anxiety around it and could easily think about something else, it's unlikely you're being compulsive. Thinking about something or fantasizing about someone is completely normal behavior and is not a compulsion on its own. On the other hand, *rumination*, that endless analysis of the mind, feels like an absolute need to solve a question at all costs. It feels like an all-hands-on-deck response rather than a recreational mental romp. If you feel urgency around the thought and if the idea of not thinking about it causes anxiety, it's likely you're engaged in need-based thinking and have identified a compulsion that should be addressed using ERP.

Likewise, it's normal to seek the approval of those we trust when dating someone new, just as it's normal to turn to friends and family during times of conflict in a relationship. Seeking support only becomes compulsive reassurance seeking when it begins to feel more like an endless search for validation that no amount of support can solve. If you find that no internet search, piece of advice, therapist, or theory is ever enough to fix your relationship anxiety or check the box in your mind, you're probably engaging in a compulsion to address with ERP.

Need-based behaviors are problematic because they reinforce the idea that we couldn't cope with discomfort on our own, that we simply *must* have an answer and could never live a meaningful life without knowing what's right. Put simply, need-based behaviors are an emotional crutch. Want-based behaviors, on the other hand, are psychologically flexible; we don't have to do them to feel okay. Ultimately, you don't need to change everything about your life to manage your ROCD, and there might even be compulsions you decide not to challenge. It's best to target the places in your life where rigid, need-based behaviors are calling the shots and keeping you from the connection and love you crave.

As you learned in chapter 1, ROCD compulsions may take the form of overt compulsions (like counting), avoidance, reassurance seeking, and mental compulsions (problem solving). The common ROCD compulsions and examples listed here may help to jog your memory, as you think about which of your own behaviors you most want to target with ERP.

## COMMON OVERT COMPULSIONS IN ROCD

- Engaging in counting rituals to ward away bad luck in your relationship

- Tapping surfaces, tapping your toes, or moving in a ritualized way around your home to keep bad things from happening in your relationship or to neutralize negative thoughts

- Washing hands or performing any other observable ritual to keep bad things from happening in your relationship

## COMMON AVOIDANCE BEHAVIORS IN ROCD

- Avoiding intimacy for fear of not being aroused enough

- Avoiding romantic movies, books, or songs on the radio for fear of being triggered

- Avoiding statements of commitment for fear of not being 100 percent certain

- Avoiding attractive people who might trigger questions about your attraction to your partner

- Avoiding talking about your relationship with others for fear that you don't sound in love enough or that others will tell you it's the wrong match

- Avoiding family gatherings, weddings, and holidays for fear of getting too involved with your partner before you are 100 percent certain of your feelings for them

- Avoiding posting about your relationship on social media for fear others will judge the relationship or that it will become "official"

## COMMON REASSURANCE-SEEKING BEHAVIORS IN ROCD

- Asking your friends, parents, or searching the internet for answers to the question "Do I love them enough?" or "Are we compatible enough?"

- Checking your partner's physical appearance, or any other form of compatibility, to test whether or not it is enough for you to stay attracted

- Asking your partner if they think the two of you are a good match or repeatedly asking "Do you love me?"

- Checking to see how you feel during sex to test whether or not you are in love/attracted/aroused enough

- Comparing your relationship to other relationships to gauge whether or not you are in the right partnership

## COMMON MENTAL COMPULSIONS IN ROCD

- Mentally reviewing how your partner looked/how they sounded/ what they said after you attend an event together, to gauge your attraction or love for them

- Mentally reviewing how the two of you met to ascertain if you had the right kinds of feelings toward your partner

- Ruminating on your feelings for your partner or analyzing if you have the right feelings in your relationship

- Fantasizing about being in another relationship; being nostalgic about a past relationship where you believe things were or would be perfect

By now, you probably have a pretty good idea of the compulsive behaviors that you want to address with ERP. You probably also have a good idea of what situations in your life are most likely to trigger these behaviors, the ones that keep you from vulnerability and risk in your relationship. Remember the goal of ERP is to challenge yourself to risk closeness and intimacy in your relationship, and to eliminate all compulsions that would neutralize your fears or to water them down so that they are easier to tolerate. ERP is all about facing our fears head-on so we can walk through them and learn that we can cope. The next step is to come up with your very own exposure hierarchy.

**EXERCISE:** Take a piece of paper and start making a list of anxiety-producing situations, or scenarios that would cause your anxiety to spike. (You can also download a blank exposure hierarchy at http://www.newharbinger. com/47919.) Organize this list of triggering situations from least to most anxiety producing, scoring each situation on an anxiety scale of 1 to 10 to represent how anxious you would feel in that situation. Use a score of 1 to represent the least anxiety-producing situation and a score of 10 to indicate the hardest exposure on the list. For example, it might feel like a 3 out of 10 to plan a date night and a 6 out of 10 to plan a vacation with your partner, but it would be a 9 out of 10 to go engagement ring shopping.

When completed, your exposure hierarchy could look like the example in figure 3.

# Exposure Hierarchy

| Anxiety Provoking Situation | 1-10 Anxiety Scale |
| --- | --- |
| Looking at images of an ex | 3 |
| Planning a date night | 3 |
| Sending a committed text such as "I love you" or "You make me so happy" | 4 |
| Excessively googling for answers to questions like "How do I know my partner truly loves me?" or "How to know you are with 'The One.'" | 4 |
| Watching romantic comedies | 5 |
| Creating and listening to a playlist of love songs | 5.5 |
| Making plans for or buying tickets for a future trip together | 6 |
| Posting an emotional or effusive social media post about your relationship | 7 |
| Moving in together | 8 |
| Going engagement ring shopping | 9 |
| Getting married, making a lifetime commitment | 10 |

Figure 3. Exposure Hierarchy

With your hierarchy assembled in order of intensity like the one in the figure, you are prepared to begin the climb to the top! You're ready to challenge anxiety and overcome ROCD through graduated exposure and response prevention. The best part is that you don't have to work your hierarchy perfectly to start seeing improvement; that's not what matters most. In fact, you can mess up, fall into compulsive behavior from time to time, and even backtrack some days, if that's what it takes to keep going. The most important quality to success isn't a straight hike to the top of the mountain; it's the attitude of willingness with which you climb.

## Working Your Hierarchy

You don't have to do it perfectly, and you don't need to feel good about it, excited, or even ready to start ERP. You only have to be willing. What does it mean to be willing? Willingness is an attitude of openness; it's a choice to take a leap of faith into the unknown without protecting yourself from the possibility of pain. You won't know that you're actually safe until you take the leap, but leap you must if you want the freedom you seek.

I frequently tell clients that the single-most important factor to anxiety management and recovery is the willingness to do what it takes. At the same time, you don't need to be *ready* to be willing. The beauty of ERP is that you gain confidence as you climb, and you don't need to know exactly how you'll get to the top. All you need, to begin working your way up your exposure hierarchy and challenging your fears, is the willingness to do what it takes and the bravery to feel afraid and step forward into the unknown anyway.

**EXERCISE:** Start with the easiest thing to tackle on your exposure hierarchy, something you rated as a 2 or a 4 on your scale of 1 to 10. It could be something like listening to a song you've been avoiding or refraining from nitpicking your partner's choice of fashion or hairstyle as you typically would. A gentle start is crucial to avoid feeling overwhelmed, and managing this step will boost your confidence. Now listen to the song if that's the place you want to start, or refrain from nitpicking if that's your choice. Do nothing else besides feel your anxiety as it rises and naturally resolves, training your brain that the threat (the one that your anxiety is trying so hard to protect you from) is neither significant nor intolerable.

What should you do while you sit there tolerating anxiety? Grab your toolbox! Use cognitive restructuring to remind yourself that *Just because I feel like I can't cope with this fear doesn't mean it's true.* Or lean in by saying something like *Absolutely, brain, you know me so well! This love song is going to be the moment I realize I never truly loved my partner at all and just married them because I was scared of being alone.* You can name the thought or feeling by saying *I'm having the thought that this anxiety will never end,* or you can take a deep breath, relax your body, and engage in a values-based action. Which tool you employ is less important than the purpose of that tool: to help you increase your willingness to sit with anxiety and let it pass all on its own; to stop fighting and to rewire your relationship to anxiety and discomfort. To do something drastically different.

Your toolbox is always available to help you face an exposure, but if the tools don't work and don't seem to increase your tolerance, no problem! You can just sit there and feel your feelings until they pass. You can weather the storm, even if you don't like the rain. There are few experiences more empowering than tolerating anxiety and recognizing that you can feel big, uncomfortable feelings while doing *absolutely nothing* except waiting for them to pass all on their own. And pass they will. They always do.

When you've successfully weathered your anxiety in this situation, call it a day and celebrate! It's a big deal to face your fears, no matter how small they may seem. Just be ready to get back in the game the next day, and the one after that, *and* the one after that, because success with ERP is all about repetition and consistency. You'll know it's time to graduate to the next level of your hierarchy when your anxiety becomes tolerable or even boring at the level you're on. If you realize what was once a 6 out of 10 now feels more like a 3 or less, it's time to move on to the next exposure. This process of exposure and response prevention continues like this until you reach the highest rungs of your hierarchy, the exposures that you've feared the most.

## Climbing Tips

Reaching the height of your hierarchy can take weeks, months, or even years; it all depends on your willingness to feel discomfort and the pace at which you choose to climb. There's no right way to climb and no right timeline, only the time and pace that keeps you moving forward in search of freedom from anxiety and ROCD.

Along the road, you will inevitably stumble. You'll experience setbacks that leave you feeling helpless, angry, and even hopeless, wondering how and if you'll ever make it through. Some exposures may feel especially difficult, and there will be days when giving up seems like the only answer. There will be days when throwing in the towel on ERP, and maybe even on your relationship, seems like the only solution to your pain. I know you'll feel this way because I walk this road with clients every single day, and I know just how hard it can be.

Here are two basic truths about ERP: one, there's no shortcut up this mountain. Earning freedom from anxiety is a long, hard road. Two, no matter how painful, the road is a worthwhile one, a journey that will transform you along the way. Eventually, if you can work all the steps of your hierarchy, you'll find you *can* tolerate all the situations, thoughts, and feelings you fear. You'll learn you're strong enough to cope, no matter what the outcome. Most surprisingly, you might find that you prefer the version of you that emerges from the other side of fear, the version of you that faces challenges head-on and doesn't wait for anxiety to call the shots. It's this evolution that legendary Buddhist teacher Pema Chödrön describes when she says, "Only to the extent that we expose ourselves over and over to annihilation can that which is indestructible in us be found" (1997, 9).

All this talk of climbing is a little exhausting, isn't it? Here are some ways to make the road just a little bit easier.

## MODULATING EXPOSURE WEIGHT AND REPETITION

You'll probably be able to jump right into the easier exposures on your hierarchy without needing to make adjustments, but as you move to the upper levels, you might notice more hesitation in your willingness to practice ERP. Rather than pausing altogether, you can modulate the weight of the exposure and number of repetitions. That is, you can make the exposure less intense and do it less often initially to increase your chance of success. For example, if you've been avoiding initiating sex with your partner for fear that you won't be aroused enough, it can seem overwhelming to make your exposure "initiate sex four times this week." Forcing yourself into an exposure that feels too intense and overwhelming can be traumatizing and can contribute to a feeling of failure that might derail your climb altogether. The goal of graduated ERP is to take it slow and steady, not to dive right into the deep end of the pool.

So if an exposure feels too big, you might choose to do something less challenging. You could start by initiating a deep kiss or foreplay but stop before having sex (adjusting weight). Alternatively, you could initiate sex but only challenge yourself to do it once per week rather than four times (adjusting reps). As you gain confidence at that level, you can add greater weight or more repetition until you reach the full exposure. Never be afraid or ashamed to modulate an exposure to make it doable; it's your willingness that matters most.

## POSTPONING YOUR RESPONSE

Another trick to tackle your hierarchy is a strategy called *postponing the response*. It involves exposing yourself to the fear, but rather than entirely eliminating your compulsive response, you simply postpone engaging in the compulsion for a fixed period of time. For example, let's say you find it incredibly triggering when your partner hasn't complimented you for a day or two. This triggers a fear that your partner might be upset with you or that they are falling out of love, causing you to check on the temperature of the relationship multiple times a day. If you cannot commit to cutting the checking compulsion altogether, then postponing it would be a great way to still be successful.

To effectively postpone your response, you first recognize that you've been triggered and then allot yourself a set amount of time to refrain from compulsively checking if your partner really loves you. The set amount of time could be ten to twenty minutes: however long it might take for your anxiety to crest and begin to subside. After you've waited the full period of time, decide if you'd like to ask for reassurance or not.

Often by simply postponing the response, you'll notice you've passed the worst of your anxiety spike and don't feel the same urgency to give into the compulsion. If you realize the need to check isn't as pressing, simply move on, and the exposure will have been a total success! But if you still want to check at the end of twenty minutes, allow yourself to do so. The time you spent denying your anxiety the relief it wanted is an important message of rebellion: you're still winning.

## ACCESSING SUPPORT

Going through ERP is a difficult process that asks you to reach deep into your reserves of strength and courage, and it's healthy to look for support as you work through your hierarchy and experience the emotions that come with it. Often the best support system will be a therapist who specializes in ERP or an OCD support group where you can speak with others going through the same journey, but support can also be found in partners, friends, or family members.

To access support in a healthy way and to avoid reassurance seeking, you can share the *process* of what you're going through rather than the *content*. Seeking support on the process of ERP sounds something like "I just did a super hard exposure, and I'm really anxious right now! I don't want to share the content of my fear, because that's unhelpful, but it would be amazing if you could hold me while I calm down." Asking in this way is completely different from sharing the exact content of your exposure, which can easily become a slippery road into reassurance seeking.

Also, let's be real, sharing ROCD content is often flat-out hurtful to your partner, and very few people would have the strength to hear your doubts 24/7 about your love or attraction to them. When it comes to family members, content can be confusing, and without proper understanding of ROCD, your friends and family could inadvertently trigger you. But when you share your process—the mechanics of what's going on, not the specifics—you allow your support team to be involved in your recovery without needing them to eliminate discomfort, which would negate the exposure altogether! Ultimately, the best kind of support doesn't solve your anxiety for you. Rather the best kind supports you while you learn that you can tolerate anxiety quite well, all by yourself.

## ERP in Action

ERP can be difficult to get in theory, so let's take a look at what it might look like in practice. Paloma's story is a good example:

> Paloma had been with Clint for five years. She is in her early thirties and has a successful career in corporate recruitment, while he is a graphic designer who works from home and loves to cook. They live together and share a dog; it's pretty clear their lives are well intertwined. And lately, Clint has been asking more insistently about the future. Paloma tells me, "I knew this was coming, but I had no idea I'd be this scared. Clint is a family guy, the type to get married, have kids, and do the whole thing. I thought I was too, but these days it's hard to feel good about all that. Clint is a great guy and a wonderful partner, but imagining our future together freaks me out!"
>
> Paloma knows she loves Clint and wants to take the next step in their relationship, but thinking about marriage and kids makes her feel trapped. She's afraid she might end up stuck in a loveless relationship with no way out, an obsessive concern that has led Paloma to avoid committed actions and steps in her relationship with Clint from the very start. Paloma avoids attending weddings for fear it will spike her own commitment anxiety, finds it difficult to openly express her feelings about Clint with her friends, and never watches movies or listens to songs that express strong sentiments of certainty, as this makes her doubt her own relationship even more. When Clint says, "You're my soul mate, Paloma. I want to spend the rest of my life with you!" Paloma responds with a watered-down "I love you, too" rather than run the risk of committing to the wrong person, or to someone she isn't 100 percent sure about. As much as she wants

*love and connection, she avoids giving too much of herself to Clint or to their relationship, holding the escape hatch open, should a better, more certain option appear.*

Before you judge Paloma (or yourself) too harshly, remember that her actions are the result of fear and that what looks like selfishness is really part of a deeply rooted psychological defense. From the outside, it's easy to look at Paloma's lack of commitment and see her as the villain in this story, but if we understand her hesitancy as a deep-rooted fear of vulnerability and loss, perhaps we can have more empathy. Paloma avoids commitment because she is terrified that she will experience regret or pain in the future. The possibility of pain and her fear that she won't be able tolerate it combine to produce powerful avoidance behaviors that block her from the quality of relationship she truly wants. By avoiding commitment, she unknowingly sends the message to her brain *I can't possibly feel scared and still move forward.* But of course she can, and so can you.

## Fear of Regret

Among the many reasons you might be hesitant to face your fears head-on is the possibility of regret. Studies have shown that a lower tolerance for regret translates to less risk tolerance, which then increases ROCD symptoms (Doron and Derby 2017). You might worry that if you drop your guard, give up your safety behaviors, and allow yourself to grow closer to your partner, you will be making a grave mistake. Many worry that they will be missing out on another, more perfect option, so they keep the door slightly open. They remain in the shallow end, hoping certainty will come before they are asked to fully dive in. The looming possibility of regret is a major hindrance to recovery in all themes of OCD, and no one likes to feel like they made a life-altering mistake! But like Paloma, your goal is not to find the most perfect match in the world, but to take the risk of love with an imperfect but *perfectly good enough* partner and then trust that, no matter what happens, you can cope with the outcome of that choice. Ultimately, the greatest risk of all is losing out not on The One, but rather on the years of life and connection lost while searching for it.

Ask yourself which is worse, a broken heart or an impenetrable one?

Like Paloma, you probably know that you want commitment and can imagine it happening with your partner but also want to be absolutely certain. But if you have an anxiety disorder, then waiting for certainty is a trap. You might never feel 100 percent certain, especially about making important commitments in your life, like becoming engaged, getting married, or having children, and no matter how happy these commitments may be, you still might feel scared. The thing is, we don't need to be certain we will have a happily-ever-after story with our partner to move forward; we only need to be certain *enough*.

*To challenge her avoidance behaviors, Paloma watches romantic comedies twice a week for one month. She also practices listening to love songs on her commute to work every day while not engaging in any compulsive behavior, like skipping past the triggering tracks or comparing her relationship to the fictional one in the song. As she moves up her exposure hierarchy, Paloma sends "cheesy" text messages to Clint. One day she sends a text that says, "You're the love of my life," and then sits in a ball of discomfort waiting to feel trapped and stuck (she does, and then that feeling passes). As ERP progresses, and she gains more confidence, Paloma and Clint attend a wedding together, and Paloma leans into her fear of never having that level of certainty in her life. When the worries arise, she actively leans into them: Oh well, brain! I guess that kind of love story just isn't in the cards for me!*

*Once Paloma is able to bring the low- and mid-level exposures down to size, she graduates to the upper levels of her hierarchy. Here, she initiates conversations with Clint about what their future might look like and even plans a day to go condo hunting. Along the way, Paloma has better days, where her willingness is high and she breezes through exposures, and other days where she feels overwhelmed and exhausted by the work. But through ERP, Paloma eventually realizes that her anxiety is an elaborate psychological smoke screen meant to distract her from the truth: that her deep love for Clint makes her incredibly vulnerable and that her avoidance behaviors keep her "safe" but ultimately alone. She finds freedom not by eradicating that vulnerability but by empowering herself to tolerate and love through it. And over time, she comes to see that the loveless, regretful life she so desperately fears is far more likely to occur through avoidance than through engaging fully with the life she has chosen.*

Paloma's is an ERP success story, and yours can be too.

## Are We There Yet?

Recovering from an anxiety disorder is not for the weak of heart. It takes daily commitment to do that which scares you most and a sort of learned masochism to get to the other side. But recovery is absolutely possible. And like a gymnast who needs to stay flexible to avoid injury and maximize success, you will need to consistently stretch your willingness muscle to keep anxiety in check. This means living with an *exposure mindset*, a recognition that as a human being, and one with an especially vigilant mind, your instinct will always be to tighten up and become compulsive when triggered.

Staying open and vulnerable is counterintuitive, but it's the exact medicine we need to treat our tendency toward hypervigilance in relationships. So it's important to make space daily or weekly to check in with yourself and ask, *Where am I getting tight this week? Where am I closing off to the possibility of vulnerability today, and what can I do to open back up?* You can add a question like this to your morning meditation or consider journaling at the end of the night. And if you find that you've gotten rigid or returned to compulsive behavior, don't be hard on yourself! Just create a plan to address it through ERP and get back to a place of acceptance and openness.

You might feel a bit overwhelmed as you consider this lifelong task. You may ask, why don't others have to put in this much work to maintain a relationship? It's true, not everyone has to be as diligent as you do in this arena, because not everyone has your unique combination of nature and nurture. But anyone who desires fulfillment must in one way or another overcome the unhelpful instincts that threaten to keep their lives small and unlived. Learning to turn toward what you fear is a hidden gift, a call to define what you want and believe in and then fight for it. ROCD might not have been the challenge you wanted or ever expected, but here it is: the call of a lifetime, a portal beckoning you to be braver than you ever imagined, to fully engage in the human experience. To be brave, you don't need to feel confident or certain; you only need to allow fear to exist and be willing to move forward anyway. Because real bravery, the hallmark of a life well lived, is living and loving in the face of fear, discomfort, and doubt.

It's how we come to see difficulty and pain not as something that makes us uniquely flawed, but as part of what it means to be fully human and, thus, fully alive.

# CHAPTER 7

# Healing Shame in ROCD

When your brain produces painful, horrifying, and taboo thoughts, as it does in OCD and ROCD, it's hard to feel normal. It's hard not to feel like you're going crazy. It's hard to stop feeling like a selfish monster who doesn't deserve love and maybe doesn't even deserve help. Feeling this way, it makes sense that we want to hide what we're going through from others. We don't want them to see beneath the exterior, to glimpse our deepest fears about ourselves: that we are damaged and abnormal; that something is fundamentally wrong with us.

Shame and its cousin guilt often show in anxiety disorders and ROCD and can make you feel uniquely bad and unlovable. Clients come in every single day and share in hushed tones fears and worries that they dare not share with anyone else in their lives, not even their closest friends and family. They worry that they are alone in the kinds of thoughts they have about their relationship, and that these thoughts mean they'll never be happy or that they're not meant for love. They come with deep anxiety that if anyone else knew how they felt or what they thought, that if anyone could see what *actually* goes on in their head, rejection would be imminent and deserved. Because so often, beneath intrusive thinking, gut-wrenching anxiety, and worries that *I just don't love my partner enough* lives an even deeper fear, one that cuts to the very quick of our primal fears of abandonment and disconnection: *What if I'm not enough?*

For many, ROCD is not only about keeping distance from another person, because we fear they aren't the right match for us, but also about the terrifying possibility that *we* are not the right match for *them*, that we are fundamentally flawed and unworthy of love. As a therapist, I'm sometimes the first person to hear these secret fears, stories of shame that have been buried deep down for decades and covered up with psychological defenses, left in the wake of failed relationships. When it comes to shame, we'll go to almost any length to avoid showing others the parts of us that we think are unworthy or flawed. But holding on to shame isn't just inaccurate; it's actively harmful to recovery. Studies show that individuals with OCD are more likely to believe that they are "mad, bad, or dangerous" and that these fears contribute to maladaptive coping mechanisms like the compulsion and avoidance behaviors that keep ROCD alive (Doron 2020). Identifying and healing any shame you may have is therefore a critical component to recovery because if left unexplored, shame becomes pure fuel for your ROCD.

But what exactly is shame, and how do we identify it?

## Identifying Shame

People often confuse and conflate the emotions of guilt and shame, which are two related but significantly different human experiences. Guilt is the feeling that *I've done something bad*, a reflection of our behaviors, while shame is a reflection of our character, a deeper feeling that says, *I haven't just done something bad. I am fundamentally bad.* Ultimately, both guilt and shame keep us from connecting with our partner because when we feel like we've messed up or *are* messed up, we'll do anything to keep our true selves from being seen or found out. But the irony is that these emotions didn't evolve to isolate people. Rather, they evolved to do just the opposite: to keep us connected! In our ancestral environments, which molded our psychology, interdependence on the tribe was a matter of life or death. Fitting in with those around us carried much higher stakes than it does today, and while our world has dramatically shifted, a sensitivity to our place and position in the proverbial tribe remains fixed. Whether our fears of rejection are rational or not, we have evolved to be sharply attuned to our sense of belonging vis-à-vis those around us; we all want to fit in.

Guilt and shame modulate this connection; they tell us when we're behaving in ways that could be dangerous to our chances of being accepted. But while the sickening gut punch of guilt is undeniably horrible, *doing* something bad can be less damaging to our sense of worth than the complete character assassination of fundamentally *being* bad experienced in shame. Therefore, this chapter will focus primarily on the understanding and treatment of shame in ROCD. But don't worry. If you experience excessive guilt, this chapter will still serve you. As you learn to recognize your own shame story and heal it through self-compassion, you may notice that feelings of guilt will resolve as well. You may notice that by treating your mistakes, flaws, and even your unwanted anxiety with kindness and compassion, everything about the quality of your life and relationship will benefit.

Shame in ROCD sounds like:

- *No one else has to go through all this to be in a relationship. Something must be terribly wrong with me.*

- *I keep causing the same arguments and falling into the same patterns! When will I stop being such an idiot and learn my lesson?*

- *Of course he broke up with you. You deserve it for having such messed up thoughts and feelings.*

- *She should just call it a day and file for divorce. I'm too damaged to make a relationship work, and I'm just holding her back.*

Believe it or not, shame is not just a toxic emotion sent to torture us and destroy our relationships. When shame functions in an adaptive way (as *healthy shame*), it serves as a warning signal for unhelpful group behavior and keeps us accountable. Healthy shame reminds us to apologize if we've hurt or cheated someone, to reflect on qualities like selfishness or stinginess that aren't winning us any fans or getting us where we want to go. It's when shame is left unchecked, unexplored, and unhealed—when it is left to fester—that it forms a wedge between you and those you love.

Like a bite of sandwich lost and forgotten beneath your car seat, it's not a problem at first, but give it a couple of weeks and the whole car reeks! Just clean out the car, right? That's the idea. But unlike deep cleaning a Toyota, healing your shame can be incredibly triggering. And it is the rare person who has the bravery to dive into themselves to rescue the pieces of their soul left behind in their childhood, the pieces they were told weren't good enough, weren't lovable or pleasing enough, to be shown to the world. Because that's exactly what happens when we are shamed as children: we split off the pieces that don't work in the environments in which we were raised. Except these pieces can't actually be discarded; they have nowhere to go! We can't just say, "Mom doesn't like that I have needs for her time and attention that she can't fulfill, so I guess I'll just give those needs up entirely." We can't just snap a finger and cut out parts of ourselves to make others feel comfortable.

## How Shame Festers in ROCD

What happens to these pieces, the parts of us that were not welcome in our childhood homes and in our society at large? We do with them what anyone would, given the problem of an offending object in the home. We hide them in the closet. We take all the parts of ourselves we are ashamed of, all the pieces that were offensive to the people we so desperately wanted to be connected to, and we hide them, hoping never to have to deal with them ever again! This strategy works quite well as long as no one gets too close, as long as you never really let anyone in for a solid look around your heart and soul. So you date unavailable partners or people whose opinion you never cared about in the first place. You spend your time avoiding intimacy and true love, favoring partnerships and situations where there is no real risk of being found out, no risk that someone will move in and eventually discover the secret closet beneath the stairs where you've stashed the unacceptable pieces.

Then, as luck would have it, you meet someone who could. This person, try as you might to stop them, steals your heart and triggers your ROCD, your psychological protective mechanism against vulnerability.

The closer they get, the closer they are to learning your secret, and the closer you feel to imminent rejection and abandonment. This is all far too triggering, and so you keep this person at a distance. You fear fully inviting them into your heart and your world because you know that eventually, if they really look around, they'll see it. If you drop your guard, if you truly relax into love and vulnerability, they'll see the discarded parts you've hidden in the closet, the parts you're absolutely sure will be the end of the relationship anyway. So why even bother? What a bind! The more you love someone, the more likely you are to fear them ever getting close enough to see the real you. The less you let someone see the real you, the less space there is for love and intimacy to grow.

That bind looks something like this:

*Marie, a bright and highly creative woman in her twenties, met and started a relationship with Jared. The relationship moved fast; the two appeared very much in love and within months had already travelled extensively together and made promises and plans for the future. Jared knew that Marie became anxious at times, and he had expressed plenty of support, but several months into their relationship, she still had not mentioned to Jared anything about her history in therapy or her diagnosis; she had not revealed that she struggled with ROCD. "He's so loving and kind," she said one day in session, "and I can't help but feel like a completely horrible person in contrast. I always say, 'I love you, too,' even though I've spent all day thinking the worst thoughts about his appearance and personality, the meanest things you could imagine! I'm despicable for thinking these things."*

*As their love grew, so too did Marie's anxiety. She felt trapped, both wanting to be honest in her relationship and feeling terrified that being honest about the process (not the exact content) of her thoughts would lead to her losing the very love she so valued: "If he knew how complicated I am, how could he ever want a future with me?" This unhealed shame was keeping Marie from revealing her true self to Jared, compromising the quality of their connection at a time when she would like nothing more than to be close.*

Marie grew up in a home where she always felt like the black sheep for her sensitivity and anxiety, and thus internalized a fear that her true nature was confusing, overwhelming, and unlovable. Her family treated her anxious spirals with disdain, and she was often left with the feeling that her emotions were a burden to those around her. As an adult, she struggles to view her OCD as just part of the way her brain functions and is consumed by the fear it's a part of her that no one could love, a flaw in her character. If you are like Marie in this way, your ROCD functions to protect you from not only the vulnerability of loss and pain, but also the fear of being found out. It serves as protection for your deep dark secrets, the ones shame says you should never show the world.

If you don't heal your shame, you'll always struggle to let someone else into your life. You'll nitpick, distance, and sabotage your way into being alone because the closer someone gets to exploring the closet, the louder your ROCD will roar. And if you don't heal shame, a part of you will stay this way, emotionally isolated and crippled by the fear that you don't actually deserve great love when it's offered to you. You'll be stuck unconsciously resisting the very love you crave, the one you've been looking for your whole life.

Unhealed shame can be devastating. But where did this idea of unworthiness and unbelonging originate? When do our shame stories take root?

## The Rules of Normalness

You, like everyone else you know, have been awash in the rules of normalness your entire life. Largely unconscious, these messages about what is right, wrong, acceptable, or immoral have been reinforced thousands of different times in thousands of different ways, through parenting, culture, religion, and the media. By the time you reached adulthood, you would have been fully indoctrinated into the cult of what's normal. You would have known what a normal body should look like, what a normal life should look like, and what a normal relationship should look like.

These messages are usually imparted implicitly—you learned by watching, not by being told—so they often exist (and power shame) outside of your awareness. But though the programming is stealthy, the rules of normalness are actually quite easy to find! Just open any social media app and scroll its feed for a moment or two. If social media isn't your thing, then watch almost any movie or listen to pretty much anything on Top 40 radio, and you'll see the rules, plain as day but never explicitly stated. These rules of normalness reflect our society's value system, a typically white, rich, straight, and 100 percent romantically infatuated view of what our lives and relationships ought to look like. But years before you ever watched a rom-com, picked up your first fashion magazine, or signed up for Instagram, you were already being normalized. And though your caregivers may have had the best of intentions, it was in your childhood home that you first learned the rules of normalness, the ground zero of shame.

The reason shame originates in our childhood environments is that your primal goal from the moment you were born was to stay connected to your caregivers. Your goal was to stay in your caregivers' good graces at all costs, no matter which parts of you needed to be shut down or disavowed to do so. And so, like all children, you became a student of what normal meant to your family. You carefully watched what behaviors were rewarded by your caregivers and which were rejected, who was praised and who ignored. You unconsciously tuned into every single detail and adjusted your behavior to fit accordingly. In an ideal parenting environment (these are rare), parents allow their children to evolve naturally into the kind of person they are meant to be, without shaming them or judging them into their own ideas of good, bad, normal, or abnormal, but most families are far from ideal. And shame stories develop in even the best of families, so hardwired are we as human beings to the possibility of disconnection and so sensitive are we to instances when we lose connection.

Think back to what it was like growing up in your home and what the rules of normalness looked like for your family. Did you receive the message, no matter how subtle, that your anxiety made you overwhelming or difficult? If so, you probably found creative ways to minimize or shut down your sensitivity. As an adult, you could find yourself struggling to accept the full spectrum of who you are, anxiety and all, preferring instead to share with others only the parts of yourself that you think are acceptable. Or maybe you grew up in a family that swept messiness under the rug, a family that preferred not to discuss the difficult or ugly parts of life. As an adult, you may have grown into a perfectionist, one who tries everything they can to keep it together and fears the middle ground, where imperfection (and humanity) resides. These are just two examples among thousands of ways that shame stories develop, and thousands of ways we come to feel too much, not enough, unlovable, or bad. Your unique story bears the mark of your family's value system, a psychological brand that holds pain as much as it holds the pathway to healing.

Even if your childhood environment was a fundamentally validating and supportive place, simply reading a book like this might be enough to cause you to feel weird or uniquely flawed. That's because the rules of normalness imply that anyone who seeks help for a psychiatric condition or experiences fluctuations in mood and functioning must be crazy or unstable and is therefore unfit for love and belonging. Many of the amazing people I've worked with over the years have expressed fears that they would be found out by their friends, families, or even bosses for coming to therapy, while others have spent months or even years in therapy before gaining the courage to try psychiatric medications, so worried were they that taking medication would confirm their true "crazy" nature.

If you've experienced mental health stigma or even stigmatized yourself, the fault is not with you; it is with a society that has come to fear what it does not understand. The fault lies in a society that has completely separated mental health from physical health and, in doing so, has complicated access to a much-needed resource for almost one-third of its population. If you are reading this book somewhere in the United States, you might be among the 30 percent of the population in any given year diagnosed with a mental health condition (a number I'm confident is grossly underreported, in part for the very reasons we are discussing here). We fear rejection so profoundly that we hide our stories of how therapy or medication saves us, stashing these messy parts in the closet with all the other pieces of ourselves that have been labelled bad or unlovable. We don't discuss or share our shame stories with others and, in not sharing, develop a false belief we are alone and unique in our struggles, that no one else needs help from time to time or could use the support of a therapist or psychiatrist.

This couldn't be further from the truth.

## Shame Stories in ROCD

When we absorb the rules of normalness countless times, in both big and small ways over the course of our life, when we see them reflected back at us through our language, media, and culture, they ossify. They become rigid beliefs and form the structure of how we come to view ourselves. They become our shame stories: the deep dark secrets we try so desperately to keep our friends, partners, and the world from seeing.

Common shame stories in ROCD take this form:

- *I'm not worthy of or meant for love.*

- *I'm too much to handle. No one will ever be able to accept me as I am.*

- *I can never be satisfied. I'll always be unhappy.*

- *I'm fundamentally selfish and cruel.*

- *I'm sexually flawed, dirty, or deviant.*

- *My anxiety makes me crazy and sick.*

- *Being in therapy or taking medication means that something is wrong with me.*

Did any of the fears in this list resonate with you? Though they feel incredibly compelling, our shame stories are not inherently true or accurate. They are merely a reflection of a thought that has been repeated or reinforced more than others by ourselves and the world around us, such as the thought *I'm unfit for love* or *Something is wrong with me*. In fact, your shame stories are much more a reflection of who you were parented by and the society you grew up in than who you are. They are much more about your caregivers' own unresolved trauma and our unequal, patriarchal, and heteronormative society than about your true nature. Unfortunately, that doesn't stop them from becoming fodder for anxiety and ROCD. These stories convince us that the only way to be loved is to reject the parts of ourselves that have been rejected, to ensure that no one ever gets close enough to out us.

Here's the truth: you were never the problem. The problem was and continues to be a world that says there is such a thing as normal and that if you or your relationship can't meet the criteria, then you are not worthy of belonging to the club. We are not born feeling bad about some parts of ourselves while feeling proud or accepting of other parts; these biases are created and informed by the environment we grow up in. Shame, therefore, is an indicator of our sense of belonging, a barometer of how deserving we feel to be part of our family and our community. It is a barometer of how connected we are to our sense of purpose as members of a tribe, of something greater than ourselves. It is the wound of belonging.

The problem is big, but the solution can be simple: clean out your closet of shame, so there's no longer any good reason not to let love in, whether it be love from your partner or the love of the world around you. Bravely rewrite the messages of unworthiness and unlovability that lead to acts of rage, depression, and isolation, the messages that cause you to hide and disconnect from others, to shut them out and view even the most caring gestures through the lens of unworthiness: *They didn't really mean that. If they only knew my true nature, they wouldn't love me at all.* Do this, so ROCD has nothing to protect you from, no piece of yourself or deep, dark secret you need to shield from view. The love you extend to your banished pieces affects everything and everyone around you, a ripple that starts small but has the power to touch every corner of your world.

That ripple starts with self-compassion.

## The Self-Compassion Cure

Sounds transformative, doesn't it? Heal shame, reclaim your wholeness, impact the world. I'm not saying the work in this chapter alone will solve all your problems, but I *am* arguing that personal healing has profound and rippling effects. I am saying that shame work is a big deal. And yet, despite this grand promise of change, you still might find yourself shying away from doing it. Like so many of my clients, you might feel that self-compassion is just too soft and that you're letting yourself off the hook by responding to your vulnerable spots with love and kindness. Maybe it feels like being kind to yourself will lead to even more slips in the future or, worse, that you'll unleash whatever bad quality you have hidden in the closet and it will take over entirely and ruin your life. Shame work is hard because, after years spent speaking to yourself with derision and loathing, this tone might have become a habit, a particularly tough one to kick.

### Cultivating Self-Worth

Although the phrase "Love yourself" sounds wonderful, it can be an exceptionally difficult thing to do when shame is burning and you feel like the worst person in the world, when all you want to do is run and hide. One of the biggest reasons we find self-compassion so difficult is that we frequently confuse the concept of *self-esteem,* the belief that we are worthy because we do worthy things, with the concept of *self-worth,* which doesn't ask us to do or be anything special to be worthy of love and belonging. Self-esteem describes how we see ourselves through the eyes of others, how we rate our personality, success, attractiveness, or likeability. It is dependent on approval and subject to change based on where we rank vis-à-vis others. Self-worth, however, runs deeper and requires no achievements or accolades whatsoever to exist. In fact, your self-worth can be quite high even if your self-esteem in a particular arena is low! That's because self-worth honors our inherent value and worth as human beings. It honors this worth on good days and on bad ones, on days when we mess up and on days when we succeed. Self-esteem says, *You are a good and worthy person because you do good and worthy things,* whereas self-worth says, *You are a good and worthy person simply because you exist.*

It's common to feel that we should only be kind and accepting toward ourselves if we do worthy things. We believe that people who speak kindly to themselves must be those who feel good about themselves, who feel that they have done and achieved goodness and are, thus, deserving. But if you believe this, you'll always be caught up in a race where worth is conditional, where kindness toward yourself is dependent on being the most beautiful, successful, and liked. What a losing game! Instead, look to cultivate self-worth, and the achievements of those around you will have absolutely nothing to do with how you decide to treat and speak to yourself. You will learn to love yourself unconditionally, not because you did anything special to deserve it, but simply because you are as valuable and precious as any baby is on the day they are born. Being alive in this moment is the only prerequisite we need to deserve love and compassion. There's nothing more needed to practice this work, and you can start right here, right now, in all your imperfection.

You can cultivate a strong sense of self-worth by increasing self-compassion, by increasing your willingness to honor and validate your own pain, to be there for yourself in times of hardship, rather than tear yourself down. The next time you feel the burn of shame, or your brain tries to bully you with a familiar shame story of unworthiness or unlovability, answer differently. Do for yourself what was never done for you: offer unconditional positive regard and support. Be the loving and accepting caregiver you might not have had growing up, the one who sees that every single thing you do, everything you think and feel, is perfectly human and therefore perfectly acceptable.

**EXERCISE:** The next time shame pops up, follow these four steps:

Step 1: Recognize and name your shame story. (Examples: *This is the one about me being a failure at love again.* Or, *I'm having the thought that, deep down, I'm just a selfish and heartless person who deserves to end up alone.*)

Step 2: Place a hand on your heart and acknowledge your pain. (*It must be so very hard to have been told you were hurtful when you were a child and to see that story show up in your current relationship.* Or, *Even though this is just a story and not the truth, it's a tough one to hear.*)

Step 3: Speak to yourself with understanding and compassion. (*Your caregiver's pain is not yours to carry, and you are no less lovable or worthy because they made you feel so.* Or, *You are 100 percent human, and all humans make mistakes sometimes. No matter what, you are still worthy of love and belonging.*)

Step 4: Affirm that struggle and pain are human. (*Making mistakes is only human.* Or, *Experiencing failure is not the same as being a failure.*)

This self-compassion practice reinforces the truth that struggle and pain are human, and that making mistakes does not make *you* a mistake. Responding to shame in this way, with patience and loving-kindness, works far better than "bucking up" or just thinking positively because in the long term, responding in this way heals us from the core. Self-compassion expert Kristen Neff says, "The beauty of self-compassion is that instead of replacing negative feelings with positive ones, new positive emotions are generated by embracing the negative ones. The positive emotions of care and connectedness are felt alongside our painful feelings. When we have compassion for ourselves, sunshine and shadow are both experienced simultaneously" (2011, 117). Rather than spending a lifetime haunted by our shadow, we can cultivate self-compassion to help us integrate the dark and the light. By acknowledging and honoring our shame, we are released from it.

Catching and correcting ourselves before we respond with judgment, blame, or derision takes time to master; unsurprisingly, the practice of self-compassion itself may require compassion! In other words, you'll need to be gentle with yourself along the way. Remember, you don't have to get it right every time; that's just another unhelpful expectation. Rather, do the best you can to notice and challenge your shame stories, and rewrite the narrative of your worth when the opportunity arises. Maybe that opportunity is right after you've said something to your partner that you wish you could take back, or it's when you notice a particularly painful intrusive thought cross your mind. Eventually, you might begin to see that, contrary to what your brain may say, your mistakes, flaws, and imperfections aren't what separate you from others— they are the keys to the club! It is your flaws that make you most relatable, your pain that makes you most human.

## Recognizing Our Common Humanity

Think back to the last time you felt ashamed. Maybe you lashed out with anger toward someone who triggered you, toward the partner or child who stepped on the sore spot in your psychology. Do you remember what that shame felt like in your body? The burning cheeks, the desire to run and hide, or even to crawl out of your skin, anything to escape the pain? Recall how small you might have felt and how separate; how difficult it was to look your loved one in the eyes because you were so overcome with the feeling that you must be deeply flawed.

It can be hard to imagine wanting to do anything but disappear in these moments, much less to use tools and strategies or respond to ourselves with kindness. But challenging this message of separateness at the root of shame is crucial to healing. The biggest lie shame peddles is that our pain and suffering makes us abnormal, that whatever thought or feeling you had or behavior you exhibited is a sign of how fundamentally different you are from those around you: how uniquely bad you really are. But OCD diagnosis or not, we all have intrusive thoughts that sound cruel or unloving at times. We all experience fluctuations in mood and mental health. Everybody has said things at times that they don't mean and has had to struggle with the fundamental human question *Does anyone else feel the way I do?*

Being a therapist offers me a privileged view of this powerful notion, the idea of our shared pain and suffering, our common humanity. It goes something like this:

> *I start my morning seeing a client who's having a difficult week. They disclose a bad night with their partner and a subsequent fear that they'll never be able to fully manage their OCD, that they'll spend the rest of their lives stuck in an endless loop of doubt and distress. Though I am well into recovery from my own anxiety disorder and have far fewer days of this sort of distress, I know exactly what my client is feeling. So I share a time in my own recovery when I felt just as hopeless, a day when I thought I could never feel the level of peace I do today (I have hundreds to choose from). Hopefully, my client will leave this session feeling better. They will leave feeling less alone in their pain and, for lack of a better term, more normal. But the interesting thing is, so do I! Though they might not know it, by sharing their fear with me and trusting that I wouldn't reject them for their vulnerability, we both have benefited. In that moment of disclosure, we connect not only as therapist and client, but as two human beings who have suffered: we are healed by our common humanity.*

Of course, I primarily treat clients with anxiety disorders and have one myself, so there will always be similarities in our underlying experiences. But most days I marvel not at how different my clients are from one another, but at how fundamentally similar we all are: my clients to one another and I to them. I marvel at how underneath our unique histories and stories, beneath our individual defense mechanisms and preservations, we are all struggling with the same sorts of things; we are made of the same stuff. And mental health diagnosis or not, all humans struggle; all humans suffer. The universality of this fact binds us together despite our differences. It serves as a powerful reminder that, regardless of how uniquely flawed we feel in our darkest moments, our suffering is our common denominator. We're in this together.

It's important to remember this for the long road ahead. It's important to remember all the ways your pain makes you human. Because recovering from an anxiety disorder isn't easy, and there will be days when you feel like the worst person in the world, days when all you want to do is shrink up and disappear. There will be days when you want to call it quits, forsaking love and belonging altogether, and days when you'll wonder if you have the strength to keep fighting for the life you want. Meet these moments with self-compassion and kindness, and watch the whole game change. Watch as your suffering shifts from a sign of your separateness to a marker of your belonging to something far greater than the pain of the moment.

And watch as everything you've ever rejected about yourself transforms from a shameful secret to proof of your fundamental humanity and a marker of your belonging.

PART 3

# The Joy of the Unknown

# CHAPTER 8

# Managing ROCD for a Lifetime

I have a confession to make. I have clients who have been in therapy with me for years, some for the better half of a decade, and I love it. But before you think I'm offering subpar therapy or somehow intentionally keeping my clients stuck in compulsions, let me explain. Managing anxiety disorders and ROCD isn't the work of a few sessions, months, or even years; it's the work of a lifetime. And like yoga, meditation, or any other practice explored over the course of a lifetime, there will be phases and stages in your recovery, times when life is being kind and your anxiety is blissfully quiet, and times when you will need more support. It's during these tough times that my clients, many from my earliest days as an OCD specialist, will return for a few sessions to review where they might be getting tight and how to unclench their psychological fists. The cases of clients whom I see for touch-up sessions aren't any more severe than those of the ones who don't come back, and these clients aren't any less successful at recovery. They have just accepted that managing anxiety is a lifelong practice, which, like all good practices in life, is a continuous revisiting, one that reveals more about ourselves with each pass.

Viewing your recovery as a lifelong practice offers you the best chances for success because it removes the expectation (and subsequent disappointment) that your efforts will one day cure you, or that you will live without ever seeing ROCD again. Although there will be weeks, months, and maybe even years when your anxious mind is less rowdy, our ingrained tendency as humans, and especially as vigilant ones, is to scan our environment for danger. This searching tendency means you are hardwired to be extra-alert and extra-attuned to your environment and to your relationship, and this is unlikely to fundamentally change even in recovery. Being extra-attuned is part of the very fabric of your being. In fact, it's your superpower! And no therapy, medication, or mindfulness practice should eradicate it. While we'd all like to take the unhelpful edge off anxiety so that we can be functional members of our relationships and society, killing it altogether would mean giving up your extraordinary genius: your intelligence, insight, and creativity. That's because your anxiety and your greatest gifts come from the same root. They are two sides of the same coin.

That's right! Like in a superhero story, our weakness becomes our greatest strength. Studies have shown that those with higher levels of anxiety also score higher on tests of intelligence and tend to have higher IQs (Coplan et al. 2012). But I don't need a research study to know this is true. The clients I work with, who have various diagnoses but are connected by a common thread of anxiety, are the most conscientious, philosophical, and fascinating people I know. They tend to be successful and profoundly sensitive to the details of life, and many are working to change the world for the better. On the one hand, they struggle to balance out the rigidity and extremes of their thinking as well as the discomfort and pain this thinking causes. On the other hand, they are finely attuned to life; they are fully alive. To give up your anxiety (if this were possible) would mean risking losing so much of what makes your life meaningful and poignant. It would mean giving up your unique gifts.

## Recovery Is a Path

Recovery is not supposed to save you from yourself, just as it's not supposed to solve all your problems or make your relationship picture perfect. You don't need to be a different sort of person, one who is never anxious but fully healed and free from pain. You don't need to change who you are. Rather, good recovery consists of a realistic plan to meet anxiety with flexibility and grace, to manage discomfort in a way that takes the edge off your ROCD while clearing space for the acutely sensitive person beneath. And if this all sounds quite deep, that's because it is. Your recovery is a spiritual path, one that will ask you every single day of your life to gently release your grip on what you don't have control over (the presence of intrusive thoughts and the pain they cause) and focus instead on what you do (how willing are you to feel that pain and move forward anyway).

To set ourselves up for a lifetime of good recovery, we must first clarify our expectations. Good recovery is not:

- The absence of intrusive thoughts or feelings
- Absolute certainty
- Perfect consistency and lifelong stability
- The elimination of discomfort or pain
- A onetime destination

Good recovery is:

- Sometimes having bad days, weeks, or even months
- Willingness to feel discomfort
- Recognizing doubt as an experience, not necessarily the truth
- Accepting that you might never have the answer
- Living according to your values even if you don't always feel it

Most of us think of recovery as a place, a physical destination where every day is anxiety-free and every kiss feels like magic. But the truth is that recovery is much more an attitude of openness toward that which we *don't* want to feel in life. Good recovery is relating to intrusive thoughts with curiosity and rationality rather than resistance; it's the deep breath you take as you make space for the gut punch of pain that shows up right before you do something scary but important, with the knowledge that you can tolerate the pain and that it will pass. And good recovery describes an updated understanding of what love really means: not just the engulfing flames of infatuation, but the daily actions that show someone you care, even when that's the last thing you feel like doing. Perhaps most powerfully, good recovery means loving yourself exactly as you are: a complex individual who will have difficult days and emotions, whose journey might look a little different from others; a unique soul whose path will involve a closer acquaintance with pain and, thus, with the heart of what it means to be alive.

Living day to day with uncertainty and discomfort is difficult work, and it takes regular maintenance.

## The Recovery Mindset

Years ago, I had a client who owned a farm in Southern California. She had crops and livestock, most notably a herd of dairy cows that supplied milk and cheese, which she sold at her local farmer's market. As we began to discuss recovery, she made a connection I still use to this day, one that perfectly describes the ethos behind the recovery mindset and describes how to keep anxiety in check for a lifetime. "Most people see me at the market or around town and think living on a farm is all about taking care of the animals and reaping the harvest, that sort of thing," she said. "They imagine me sitting around with a blade of hay in my mouth, on a rocking chair, but they don't actually realize that most of what I do is repetitive and mundane." (I won't lie; I had imagined her life as a bucolic paradise when we first started working together.) "I love my animals, and it's rewarding to see people enjoy what we make, but behind the success of any good operation, you'll find one thing: hours of fence management."

Fence management was the key to a prosperous farm? Yes.

Of course, my client also tended to the animals and reaped the harvest: all the typical farmer tasks we see from the outside. But those enjoyable moments wouldn't be possible if she didn't prioritize the mundane and repetitive work of managing the fences, among a heap of other uneventful tasks that needed to be done to sustain her farm. Every day, my client (or one of her children or employees) had to tend to the miles of fencing surrounding her property, looking for small breaks in the wiring or holes dug around the perimeter, so the cows stayed in and the predatory animals stayed out. Fence management was not a onetime task, and my client was never done managing her fences. Rather, she had incorporated fence management as a tedious but absolutely necessary component to the health of the farm and, thus, her family. She didn't particularly love doing it, but she woke up every day and knew what needed to be done. She accepted fence management as a means to sustaining and maintaining the life she wanted, as part of what it meant to own a prosperous farm.

You don't need to mend an actual fence to take a valuable lesson from my client's story—that the life you want and the recovery you seek will require a bit of regular maintenance—to see that recovery is not a destination, but a practice of tending to the sore spots and mending the gaps day in, day out. Done diligently, the recovery mindset keeps your herd of intrusive thoughts and feelings in check. It shores up your fences and patches holes, so anxiety doesn't run wild and wreak havoc on your life and relationship. And while mending fences looks different for everyone, all good recovery includes some possibly boring but necessary tasks. Maybe your fence management looks like a meditation practice or carving out the time to exercise and get outdoors. It could be advocating for more space and rest in a busy schedule, or it could be limiting your screen time. Fence management can look like therapy with a qualified specialist, a routine of self-care, or really any of the seemingly insignificant but important ways we ground ourselves throughout the day.

Some days, twenty minutes might be all the management you need to get back to baseline. Then again, during especially stressful times, you might need to devote weeks or even months to gather up a herd of intrusive thoughts and methodically work to get yourself back on track. Regular fence maintenance makes for a prosperous farm, just as mental maintenance makes for a prosperous life, so as tempting as it is to finish a course of therapy or read through a treatment book and say, "Great! That's it then. I've done everything Sheva says, and now I'll never have to work on my mental health," good recovery takes sustained effort. Accepting what it takes to be a highly attuned individual in an anxiety-producing world is the only way to reap the harvest of life. So you've got to invest in the fence work, tedious as it may be.

The good news is that, as tedious as lifetime management may sound, every day you spend managing your mental fences, you will notice it becoming more intuitive to do so. Over time, you might barely notice the extra work it takes to keep yourself in the recovery mindset, an attitude of willingness, acceptance, and tolerance toward intrusive thoughts and feelings and toward unwanted experiences in life. But no matter how fastidious a farmer you may be, sometimes the cows will break free. You'll find yourself compulsively seeking answers, googling, ruminating, *anything* to try to escape the discomfort you're feeling and solve the urgent questions in your mind. But don't beat yourself up! This is all part of recovery. Just recognize that compulsions don't work and won't bring you the kind of mental clarity and peace you want; they aren't helpful in pursuit of your values. Gently place yourself back on the more difficult but sustainable path of long-term management; get back to the fence work.

## Good Recovery Tools

Let's start by acknowledging that some days are just plain better than others. Some days you feel stronger, more certain, and more capable of handling whatever trigger anxiety throws your way. On these days you embody the bring-it-on attitude. You feel great! Connected! In love! Those are wonderful days and should be celebrated. But there are other days when you will wake up with a brain that's spinning, and the whole world will feel dark and impossible. You won't be able to remember, for the life of you, why you ever partnered with the person sleeping next to you and won't be able to connect with a single redeeming quality in them. Believe it or not, both types of days are part of what it means to be recovered. Good recovery isn't perfect bliss and connection; again, it isn't a fixed destination reached by following the straight and narrow. Rather, recovery is a state of mind, an attitude of flexibility and willingness that keeps anxiety and ROCD in check, even on the tough days.

## See Detours as an Opportunity

The quickest way to hijack your recovery is to believe that once you feel good, you are fully recovered and should remain this way indefinitely. I see so many clients who come to therapy crestfallen and defeated after a bad week, saying something like "I'm backsliding and losing all my progress! ROCD will always get the best of me." A bad week isn't a sign of backsliding at all; it's merely a detour in the route, an opportunity to mend fences and make them even stronger than before. Like an exit off the freeway on the road to your ultimate destination, having a rough day or week (or month) with anxiety does not mean starting over from the beginning; you're still on the same trip. If you can accept that you will have thousands of detours along the way, you won't be so startled when they inevitably occur. You'll find it easier to brush off the dust and get back to work.

## Maintain Good Lifestyle Habits

The small choices you make every day might not seem like they could significantly impact your anxiety. But habits, both helpful and unhelpful ones, accumulate over time and can have a big impact on your mental health. You might find, for example, that your anxiety is much harder to manage after a few nights of poor sleep or a weekend out drinking with friends. Likewise, you might have noticed an extra cup of coffee makes you feel on edge, jumpier and more irritable. I've noticed that my anxiety is higher when I have lots of unstructured time on my hands; weekends and holiday breaks can actually make me more anxious than less. All that time to think gives my brain ample opportunity to look for anything that could be wrong, and I have to make adjustments to balance the heavier load of anxiety during these times. I might wake up earlier to meditate, see fewer clients, or prioritize alone time. I try not to get frustrated or berate myself for needing to do these things, but to just accept them as part of my maintenance strategy.

There are many lifestyle factors that can make you more susceptible to anxiety and less equipped to tolerate it, but the answer cannot be to completely organize your life to avoid stressful situations. For one thing, this is impossible to do perfectly, and you'll miss so much that's valuable if you try. It's more realistic to recognize that certain choices might trigger your anxiety and to adjust accordingly if you decide to proceed. You might, for example, know that less sleep leads to a more difficult day but choose to stay up late with your friends and family anyway! By becoming aware of what triggers your anxiety, you'll be less likely to buy into intrusive thinking when it does arise and better equipped to accept whatever emotion shows up. You'll be more likely to create space. You'll be less reactive, less resistant, and thus less affected by your anxiety, even if it does come on strong.

## Get to Know Your Triggers

Understanding which lifestyle factors contribute to your anxiety empowers you to decide what steps to take. Common lifestyle triggers include:

- Lack of adequate sleep (less than eight hours a night or interrupted sleep)

- Poor nutrition (undernourished or overly rigid and restrictive)

- Relationship conflict not primarily due to ROCD

- Excessive alcohol consumption

- Excessive or late-in-the-day caffeine consumption

- Overextending yourself socially

- Emotional burnout from parenting duties or work

- Monthly hormonal changes

- Lack of alone or restorative time or too much unstructured time

- Times of increased stress or transition

I was first introduced to the importance of transitions through the work of Sheryl Paul, a wonderful Jungian counselor and author who explores the potency of life stages and their corresponding emotional impact. She writes about how (particularly in Western, individualistic cultures) we fail to acknowledge and honor the fact that transitional moments, no matter how happy they are, can actually trigger immense anxiety and grief. Perhaps we have some understanding of how the loss of a loved one, an adult child leaving the home, or the stress of a move could bring about big emotions. But we rarely consider how even happy changes can cause our anxiety to spike. We are told that birthdays, anniversaries, graduations, and momentous events like weddings should be joyous occasions for celebration and nothing else, but the reality is that any transition is a step into the unknown, regardless of how positive that step may seem. That's why, for many of my clients and likely for you, too, transitional stages in life may be quite destabilizing. These are times when you might notice a spike in your ROCD and an increase in the presence of intrusive thoughts, even if the transition is an objectively happy occasion.

A client recently told me about how the possibility of becoming a mother made her incredibly anxious and that she found herself critiquing her partner even more with such a big life change on the horizon. Her ROCD wanted to be absolutely sure she was making the right decision moving forward into family life, since there would be no turning back. Because she felt like she shouldn't be having these feelings, she became judgmental of herself: "Everyone else would be happy to be in my shoes, so why do I feel this anxious? Does this mean I don't really want to have a child or that I just don't want one with this person?" But her anxiety made perfect sense to me. Anyone making such a significant life change might be anxious, and yet when the transition is a supposedly happy one, we become rigid with ourselves and eliminate the mental space needed to navigate the spike. We feel shame for our complex emotions, blame ourselves for them, and self-isolate even more, creating a vicious cycle that increases the turbulence during this time.

Feeling anxiety during transitions doesn't mean the direction you've chosen is wrong. Like a sensitive instrument, you're just more tuned into the complexity of change, more aware of the forks in the road of life and what it might mean to take one over another. The truth is that while graduations are a time for celebration, they are also the end of one era in your life. A wedding highlights not only the joy of finding a partner, but also the loss of your identity as a single person. Likewise, becoming a mother inevitably includes a forsaking of self-interested pursuits and a recognition that your life is no longer yours alone. How we choose to engage with the fundamental groundlessness we feel during times of transition affects the quality of our recovery.

By now, I hope to have proved that the recovery you seek, the kind that leads to deep connection, passionate intimacy, and lasting love is absolutely possible; it just might not look the way you thought it would. It's not as easy or as clean, and it's not all that fun. The word *recovery* sounds like it should be all positive, a "Yay, we made it!" experience, but the truth is that there are plenty of casualties in the recovery process. I've yet to see someone go through recovery without experiencing sadness at the thought of the deeply held wishes and desires for what they thought their life would look like, the ones they had to release along the way. All this is to say that one piece of good recovery that we often overlook involves grieving the things we didn't get, the way the story didn't turn out. We're not grieving because it's a bad story, a horror story, or a story with a sad ending. We grieve because living with anxiety is not the story we wanted or expected

Managing fences to stay connected is not what you imagined doing with your time, and not everyone will understand your struggle. Sometimes even the people closest to you won't be able to feel what it's like to have ROCD, what it's like to live with doubt as your constant companion. There are many days when you'll feel alone.

Good recovery asks that you make space for this, that you allow the experience of anxiety to change and transform you. It asks that you look at pain as a portal to living more fully, not an experience to be avoided at all costs. But before we can experience pain this way, before we can truly embrace the discomfort that will arise when we confront our lives as they are and accept our new reality, before we can get to a place where we revel in it and the wonderful things it will show us about ourselves and the world, we must grieve what we have lost.

## Make Space for Grief

To grieve something is to honor it, to acknowledge that which has passed or will never come to pass. Grieving is an action, just like loving, an active process that asks us to pause and metabolize our sadness and loss. We try so hard to avoid grieving because it isn't pleasant, but good therapy and lasting recovery always and inevitably involve multiple meetings with grief. ROCD or not, who hasn't felt deep sadness when thinking about the kind of life they thought they would have, the one without anxiety or pain, the one with the picture-perfect love story? Who among us hasn't needed a good cry from time to time when things didn't turn out the way we thought they should? Feeling sad doesn't mean you made the wrong decision or that you would trade your reality for another. It's just that growth and grief come hand in hand, and your recovery will highlight this interplay.

Good recovery always involves encounters with grief because all growth involves shedding old ways of thinking and being, while taking on new ones. Grief shows up in the loss of other romantic possibilities, the ones we silently say no to when we say yes to another. It appears in those moments in life that we think should be happy but are perforated with apprehension and fear. And it shows up when contemplating the years spent stuck in compulsion and avoidance, the time we've lost to anxiety. It's completely normal to feel grief, yet we are never really taught how to navigate it, how to feel our feelings, so we can eventually move on. Instead, you probably received messages like "You'll be fine," or "Look at the bright side" when you felt sad.

So it's no surprise that as adults we fear where grief will take us. We worry that slowing down to feel the sadness will allow it to overtake us, or that grieving is indulgent and harmful to those we love. We are so consumed with avoiding grief that we never get to explore what it's like; we rarely allow ourselves to feel what Francis Weller in his book *The Wild Edge of Sorrow* calls the "strange intimacy between grief and aliveness," the "sacred exchange between what seems unbearable and what is most exquisitely alive" (2015, 1). Because when you allow full-bodied grief in, that's what happens. You become most alive. You head into the darkness but inevitably emerge again into the light, into a greater appreciation and heightened awareness of life. The best part is that there's no such thing as the wrong way to grieve, as long as you take time and space to feel your sadness and let it work through you.

**EXERCISE:** Take a moment to acknowledge what you've lost to anxiety, without judging yourself or diminishing what that loss meant to you. You can write in your journal, share with a trusted friend, or simply take some time to acknowledge loss in whatever way or through whatever ritual makes sense. Be sure not to hurry yourself through the feelings that arise as you consider the beliefs, people, hopes, and dreams you have had to let go to be where you are today.

No matter how much I try to shoot it down, it might have been the very fantasy of MOTO that got you through some of the most difficult times in your life. It might have been the very belief that someone would appear who could take away your pain and soothe your fears. And even though the myth of perfect love no longer serves you, that doesn't mean it won't hurt to let it go. So go ahead and grieve the meet-cute moment you'll never have: where you just knew they were The One. Grieve the absolute certainty you'll never achieve in this or any relationship. Grieve the painless and seamless connection you dreamed of when you were younger, and the life free from doubt and discomfort. Grieve it all. The more willing we are to tunnel into darkness, the more brilliant the light is on the other side.

# A Walk Down Recovery Road

Something interesting happens toward the end of my time with an ROCD client. I notice that they begin to talk about the content of their fears less and, instead, describe the curious feeling of a brain that is turned on and searching for something to fixate on but can't quite seem to gain ground. By the later stages of treatment, my clients have become sharper at not taking the bait, so when their brain says *Wow, you didn't really miss him when he left, so you must not really be in love,* or tries something like *You haven't had sex in a couple of weeks—I told you there wasn't any chemistry,* they don't respond with compulsions or resistance like they used to. Instead, they begin to trust it all as hollow content. They begin to see their anxiety as all talk. Maybe they lean into the fear by saying *Yup brain! I guess I hate my partner!* and move on with their day, or they answer with self-compassion, saying something like *I can see you're having a hard day, but not everything you think is automatically true.* Whatever the strategy, they're just not biting anymore; they're not feeding into the fear machine. Without anything to catch them on, anxiety is left to search and scan, looking for something, anything at all, to rile them up, no matter how redundant or ridiculous it may be. I call this the "lighthouse effect," a term to describe the searching and endless seeking beneath the stories our anxiety tells us.

As an anxious person, you have a powerful lighthouse built up in your mind. Everyone has one, but your lighthouse has an intense light and scans the horizon tirelessly for danger, day after day. Whether built up by genetics, environment, or (most likely) both, that scanning sensation will have to be accepted rather than eradicated; you can't demolish your lighthouse. But an internal lighthouse it isn't all bad, because it's this very same system that keeps you alert, aware, and thus very much alive and highly attuned to the environment around you. In fact, your lighthouse was probably constructed in a childhood environment where being vigilant and alert served you and maybe even saved you. Perhaps the first bricks of your lighthouse were laid down in a home where you had to walk on eggshells to avoid conflict or in a family system or society that required you to hide parts of who you were, lest you be rejected. Before you even knew it, there was a strong lighthouse in your mind that tried to keep you safe, scanning the world for anything that could cause you pain.

It's amazing when clients tell me they have reached this point, where they see past the content of their thoughts and watch their brain "lighthousing." They watch with a mix of irritation and amusement as their brain spins but finds nothing to grab their attention, no sensational story of inadequacy to justify its existence. Sometimes you may wake up and notice the lighthouse going even before you've opened your eyes! Or you might notice the urge to attach a story, any story, to the feeling of anxiety and threat it produces. But as you move further down recovery road, you'll begin to notice that not all anxiety has a reason to be there; not every feeling means there is an actual threat! You can watch as your brain jumps around looking to capture your attention with the story of the day, and playfully call it out by saying something like *There goes the lighthouse! Searching for anything to try and get me. What will it be today?* Or maybe you simply notice it searching, and choose not to pay attention. You don't need to demolish your lighthouse; you only need to recognize when its frantic searching captures your attention or tries on some new, shiny piece of content, and then gently disengage.

## The Vulnerability of Joy

We've arrived at the end of this chapter about recovery. Even so, you may be feeling some anxiety at the thought of letting go of your old ways and stepping into new ones. Many people unconsciously resist recovery because they hold deep fears about what it means to feel good and to be safe. This resistance often comes from growing up in a family where you've had to live on edge, always watching what you said and how you behaved lest you lose parental approval or love. If this describes you, then feeling good and dropping your guard could have left you vulnerable and exposed to real danger. Retiring your lighthouse operator would have meant possibly saying the wrong thing or doing the wrong thing and incurring punishment or, even worse, emotional rejection. Whether you grew up in a home like this or not, recovery can be complicated because anxiety is at its core protective, and recovery asks you to step out from beneath its guard, illusory as that protection may be.

The work then, becomes to actively rewire the thought that feeling good or relaxed inevitably leads to getting hurt. To challenge, through our thoughts, behaviors, and attention, the belief that dropping our guard is stupid or naïve, and that connection to another person is dangerous. In a word, the work is to trust—not that everything will be okay but that *we'll be okay*—even if things don't end up the way we wanted them to. Trust is the exact opposite of doubt, but it has nothing to do with having all the answers. Rather, to trust ourselves is an act of faith; it is knowing that although the road is difficult and full of detours, we have the strength to cope. It is an embrace not of answers, but of the magical properties of the unknown and our ability to be transformed by them.

CHAPTER 9

# A New Kind of Love Story

At last, we arrive at the final stage of climb. The summit is within view. And while your final task may sound simple, it could prove to be the most challenging of all. To fully step into healthy love and manage ROCD for a lifetime, you must let go of MOTO. You must fully abandon that fireworks fantasy of Boy meets Girl and choose a new kind of love story altogether. This love story won't be as glamorous or as effortless, and your love won't whisk you away on a white horse or solve all your problems. But your story will be more meaningful than all that because *it will be real.* Believe me when I say it's going to be hard to break up with MOTO. Maintaining this myth is especially tempting when day-to-day living can be painful, mundane, and filled with unknowns. But the Myth of the One hasn't delivered on its promise of happily ever after. Instead, it has strangled good-enough love with an expectation of perfect partnership.

MOTO isn't just a problem for those of us with anxiety and ROCD, and it doesn't just affect people with an insecure attachment style. It's a pervasive and damaging myth that, left unchecked, has the power to strip all our relationships of their glorious pain and powerful purpose. What is that purpose, you may ask? The answer is different for everyone, but if we adhere to a single story of love and become blind to all other iterations, we'll never find out. I don't know what good love means to you, and I don't pretend to have the answer. But what I do know is that your relationship was never meant to be perfect. I know that relationships were always meant to be vehicles of profound personal and spiritual growth. And I know that often we evolve through what isn't working in our relationships rather than through what does; that through these imperfections, we find the pathway to our highest self.

Love is transcendent! Just not the way you might think. And in our new love story, the update we need to find and maintain satisfying relationships and manage ROCD, we make space for that imperfection. We clear away the unrealistic and, quite frankly, basic view of love offered to us by MOTO and the capitalistic influences that keep it alive, and we relish in complexity. We learn to live in the gray. And remember when we discussed how difficult transitions can be because they ask us to step into the unknown? This transition might be the scariest of all because our new love story isn't about pinning down a perfect formula to find and maintain love. Rather, this chapter will be all about identifying the basics of healthy love before you sail off into the unknown to build it for yourself, to define it exactly as you like.

One size does not fit all.

As you discover what good love means to you and release the need for absolute certainty in your life and in your relationship, something surprising might happen. You might feel the pain of the unknown, the very pain I've asked you to cozy up to since the start of our journey together in this book, slowly morph. Or rather, you might find that you have morphed within it. Now you do more than just tolerate the unknown: you *thrive* in it. We've spent all this time looking for an answer when the truth could be sitting right in front of us. I believe that the love you have always been searching for is right here, and that it's been here all along. It's just sitting a few steps to the left of perfect.

## What to Look for in Love

Our new love story has many of the qualities you've come to associate with the "right" relationship. But it also has concepts that might sound unfamiliar, concepts that might even offend your current romantic sensibilities. While none of the following is a guide to how to pick a perfect partner (you know I don't play that game), you can use this chapter to help construct more realistic expectations for love, connection, and partnership. Use it to correct and rebalance the unhelpful narrative of MOTO, which claims to have all the answers when it comes to love, only to leave us entirely disappointed and disconnected from it. Use this chapter to evaluate your relationship while remembering the fundamental truth, that there is no such thing as The One, just as there is no such thing as the right way to be partnered.

Disclaimers aside, the good relationships that I've encountered in my work have certain qualities in common, some of which exist at the start of the partnership and some of which grow into being. I call them the three Cs of healthy love: chemistry, connection, and compatibility. You'll recognize these qualities from all the romantic comedies, love songs, and MOTO messages you've received all your life. But in this chapter, we'll redefine them. We'll take them back from the cult of perfection and retrofit them to serve our complex modern relationships. We'll give these important qualities the update they so desperately deserve.

Let's start by redefining what it means to have chemistry in your relationship.

## Chemistry

In every good relationship I've worked with, ROCD or otherwise, there exists some kind of chemistry, some difficult-to-describe draw that pulled you toward your partner in the first place. Perhaps it was their confidence or their smile or the way they made you feel comfortable and fully seen. Maybe it was their kindness, good heart, and generosity toward others and the world around them. Whatever it was, something piqued your interest and drew you closer, a moment or series of moments revealing the possibility that this could be more than just friends. If you think of it now, you can probably name these qualities in your partner, the ones that made you want to know more about them. But unless you had the you'll-know-it-when-you-feel-it experience of certainty right from the start, you might worry something is missing from your love story. You might worry that the absence of instant fireworks could be a sign you have made the wrong choice.

That's because MOTO says the only way to claim chemistry in your relationship is if all the right feelings were there from the very start. It says the only valid way to meet is the one that takes your breath away and sweeps you off your feet. Sure, we've all had those moments, but this limited definition doesn't account for whether the person doing the sweeping is available, loving, or compatible. MOTO says it doesn't matter as long as you have that feeling, the one you were promised would be all you needed to know that you had met your soul mate. However, studies don't support MOTO. In fact, a study conducted at the University of Texas at Austin found that initial attraction correlated strongly with the likelihood of new relationships forming but had no effect on long-term marital satisfaction or success (McNulty, Neff, and Karney 2008). Or, to put it differently, that spark we feel when locking eyes with a person walking by on the street or on the first few dates is undoubtedly exciting, but it just isn't an accurate predictor of long-term success or satisfaction.

We need a new way to look at what it means to have chemistry in our relationships, a definition with lasting power. Our updated definition of chemistry can and should describe the alchemy of a partnership not just in the first few moments or months, but in the curiosity it takes to maintain a partnership for the long haul, well after the honeymoon phase has passed. It should include the indescribable pull toward your partner not only in good and easy times, when money is good, stress is low, and the world remains on its hinges, but also in tough times, when it's not pretty or easy to like one another. Of course, every good relationship has a draw, some spark of chemistry and attraction that can be kindled into a blaze. But whether this feeling was there from the moment you locked eyes or came about slowly through a buildup of trust and connection makes no difference. The chemistry that matters most is the one that makes the leap of faith toward love worth taking every single day. It's what justifies the jump.

I've probably never met you, but my guess is that you want very badly to be a part of your relationship and to feel the love you have chosen. Likewise, I don't need to know your partner to surmise that there must be something pretty special about this person, the person you're willing to fight through all the noise to reach. And I don't need to know the intricacies of your partnership to be reasonably certain that you wouldn't be here doing this incredibly difficult work, the work of transforming yourself and facing your anxiety head-on every single day of your life, if there weren't something worth fighting for beneath it all: someone to whom you are indescribably drawn. You're doing something a lot harder than just closing your eyes and relying on MOTO chemistry to make magic happen; you're putting in the work. You're doing what it takes to access the energetic attraction between you and the one you love, a force that has been there from the very beginning, buzzing patiently beneath fear.

I sense some chemistry here, don't you?

## Connection

MOTO also says that the ideal partnership is one in which the connection between two people—that cord of positive regard, mutual desire, shared interest, and can't-get-enough closeness—should remain forever unbroken. It shouldn't matter what challenges life throws at you, because if it's the right relationship, your connection shouldn't break or falter. Anything else means you have (you guessed it) settled for less or that your relationship is in danger. MOTO would like us to believe that when you find The One, you will find a person who will always know exactly what you want and how to give it to you, emotionally, physically, and spiritually. MOTO would like you to wake up every single day and feel grateful for the person sleeping next to you and go to bed every night growing deeper and deeper in love, and MOTO definitely makes no room for conflict. But most of what we do as humans doesn't occur in a perfectly straight line like this.

Take babies, for example, who grow steadily for the first few months of life and then experience sleep regressions regularly throughout the rest of their first year. Though new parents might find these regressions tedious, they understand them to be harbingers of positive change and a sign that the baby is about to enter into a new stage of growth and development. We have some patience for the cyclical nature of growth in babies, so why are we so much harder on ourselves as adults? With MOTO, moments or seasons of disconnection become dangerous signs of incompatibility, when they are actually natural revolutions in the cycle of love and connection you feel in your relationship. We think growth must be constant and consistent! But the research shows a much different truth. A study done by legendary relationship researchers John and Julie Gottman shows that we are only emotionally available in our relationships 9 percent of the time, leaving a full 91 percent of our interactions ripe for disconnection, misunderstanding, and conflict (Gottman and Gottman 2008). Interestingly, the Gottmans also found that these misunderstandings are far less important in the relationship than the repairs that follow them. In other words, a fight with your partner isn't a big deal. What matters most is how you solve it.

If disconnection is normal, then why do we fear it so much in our relationships? In many ways, our craving for connection goes back (like most things) to our evolutionary history. It goes back to our extreme vulnerability at birth, the vulnerability that makes us dependent on caregivers in ways that distinguish us from any other mammal. Human babies are incredibly helpless. When we were babies, our caregivers' only task (whether they accomplished this or not) was to recognize and respond to our many needs, to anticipate every gurgle and cry and respond with something, anything, to satisfy and soothe us. So as adults, we unconsciously crave (and have been told to expect by MOTO) this same responsiveness from our romantic partners. It makes perfect sense, then, that we are heartbroken when they can't provide it, when the reality of living with a unique other means we'll have to work to be understood and work to understand the other. We hope that, without our ever needing to explain it to them, our partner will notice when we are sad and know how to calm and soothe us. We expect them to know how to touch us in exactly the way that works for us, in a way that requires no explanation. We expect them to know our fears and to step lightly around our wounds, as if they had a map of exactly where it hurts.

The truth, of course, is that you will inevitably feel disconnected from your partner over the course of a long-term relationship. Perhaps you will feel some version of this disconnection daily, however small or silly, when they forget to load the dishwasher after you've asked them multiple times. Maybe it will be in the sting of rejection you feel if they don't find the same things as interesting or funny as you do. You will notice disconnection in bigger ways when you differ on how to allocate finances or on optimal parenting methods. Some days, you will be tired and they will be energetic. Some months they will have high desire and libido while you struggle to want any intimacy at all. Eventually, you will come to realize that your partner will never fully understand you.

They were never meant to!

Our updated definition of what it means to be in connection includes plenty of space for interruptions, misunderstandings, and differences of opinion. It leaves plenty of room for *dis*connection. And though it feels counterintuitive, this definition must include a tolerance for the thousands of cycles of rupture and repair we will experience over the course of a partnership. Our new understanding of connection must allow the natural coming together and moving apart inherent in all human relationships, not only romantic ones. It is through these breaks that we learn the most about ourselves and about the other. It is precisely in these moments that we are offered the chance to question our thoughts and beliefs, lower our defenses, bring compassion to old wounds, and thus evolve and grow into our highest selves.

When we learn to navigate these moments of disconnect successfully, we mature past the helpless children who must depend on others to do the work of vulnerability for them, who require capable adults to anticipate their every need and soothe their every fear. Your updated love story kindly asks that you stop placing this burden on your relationship, thank you! As adults, we are given the chance to have the intimacy and warmth of connection with a twist: we have to do it grown-up style. We must actively work to maintain and enrich connection, evolving from "If you love me, you should always know what I want and need" to "It's each of our responsibilities in this partnership to identify and express our needs clearly and respectfully to one another. Only then can I expect you to honor them."

## Compatibility

When it comes to finding the right match, the compatible one, MOTO makes a big promise. It says the hardest part of love is finding The One and that what follows should be easy. It tells us the arduous search you'll need to undergo to find them is worth it because the right person is to be the single person in the world destined to solve all your problems, the one who will save you from yourself. This person, your soul mate, will love you into being a better person. They will love you into recovery, they will love you into certainty, and they will love you so profoundly that you won't have to do any of the tedious, mundane work yourself; you won't ever have to feel the pain of your own vulnerability and be tasked with the responsibility of your own growth. According to MOTO, perfect compatibility is more than just having similarities or complementary differences. It is a grand promise of painless living, the promise that if only you search long and hard enough, the prize that awaits you is the greatest of all: an escape hatch from human suffering.

That's quite the promise! But painless partnership is exactly what MOTO sells us on. Except, of course, no partner on earth, not even the most wonderful, can take away the true purpose of your relationship, which is not to be saved by another person but rather *to grow with and as a result of* the other person. The goal is to see our relationships not as vehicles for salvation from our lives but as, what relationship therapist and author David Schnarch calls, "people growing machines" (1997, 140). I couldn't think of a more perfect way to reorient ourselves toward the goal of healthy love, a more perfect mission statement for our updated love story, than to view our relationships as our greatest teachers.

So often when we look for someone who is compatible, what we are really looking for is a partner to do for us what we aren't willing to do for ourselves. We want them to make us feel loved when we don't love ourselves. We want them to make us feel desired when we won't take the time to explore ourselves first. We ask them to be so irresistible and perfect in every single way so that we never need to overcome our own fear of vulnerability and closeness, so perfect that we never need to turn toward doubt and discomfort and become our best selves by facing those feelings head-on.

The goal of healthy partnership and compatibility has always been to support you along the path of your own actualization, not to save you from it. The compatible partner, the one you should look to find and to become, is the one who will stand by you through life's challenges, not erase them with a dazzling smile. The compatible partner is the one who has the willingness and commitment to put in the necessary work required to grow *with* you, not for you. Don't allow MOTO to reduce your understanding of compatibility into a tasteless story of savior and saved, of lost and found, the kind that sells movie tickets and inspires teen fantasy. While it's true when they say that love can make you move mountains, we rarely think of those mountains as the blocks inside ourselves, the ones that keep us chained in toxic patterns of behavior and protection. We rarely see that the biggest mountains to be conquered have nothing to do with the outside world and everything to do with the quiet battles we wage inside ourselves.

## What Not to Look for in Love

Redefining the three Cs of healthy love, or what it means to have chemistry, connection, and compatibility in your relationship, is an excellent start, but it's just the beginning; the rest is up to you. To reclaim love as one of the most transformative vehicles in the human experience, adding color, texture, and depth to its definition, you've got to get comfortable with the gray areas. You've got to resist the neat and tidy definitions of what makes love good, right, or true, the stories that fit into a two-hour movie or a two-minute love song. As you layer on complexity, however, an old friend will likely make an appearance. That's right! Your ROCD will have something to say about all the remodeling going on upstairs. That's because ROCD wants you to stay safe by staying small, and it will do anything it can to steer you away from a more complex (read: accurate) view of love and partnership in favor of the fantasy version. It will tell you that everything you do to unravel MOTO is because you're in denial. Let it talk. Let it say anything it wants. You have more important things to do than listen; you're busy sparking a revolution.

Toss MOTO out and become the resistance. Champion every manifestation of love and partnership, no matter how it started or how closely it aligns with the movie kind. Resist judging your relationship or the relationships around you—just because they look or don't look a certain way—so you can relax into the love story in front of you, not one dreamt up in a studio. Healthy love and partnership require that we take on many new ideas, ideas we've discussed throughout this book, ideas like the three Cs. But it also requires plenty of *undoing*, plenty of unlearning the damaging messages that have led us to the state of relationships we see today, where many fail and even fewer are truly satisfying. We've spent a lot of time discussing what to look for in love, but part of our unlearning means we need to explore *what not to do* as well.

So if you're looking for healthy love and partnership...

## Don't Trust Your Gut

To experience satisfaction in your relationship and to effectively manage your ROCD, you *must abandon completely* the belief that your emotions alone will lead you to the right partner or that they will be accurate indicators of whether you should stay or leave. Everything about MOTO values heart over head, emotion over rationality, but picking a partner and committing for life is too important a choice to leave to something as ephemeral and petulant as our feelings. Remember that our gut is a microphone for our mind, and if you are a highly attuned person with a sensitive threat response, fear messages will sound louder and more convincing than anything else you might be feeling. They will sound louder than love, louder than attraction, and louder than the desire to commit. Remember that what we feel to be true is often an indicator of what we *fear* to be true, so no matter how many times your friends and loved ones will advise you to "trust your gut" in relationships, don't listen.

Of course, we don't need to throw away our emotions; they are valuable data points that can and should be considered when moving through the world. But they cannot be the only indication of what does or doesn't work in a relationship. This morning you might have felt sad, and now you don't. Last month you felt confident and capable; this month you are filled with doubt. No one who loves you would advise you to make any other major decision in life based off emotion alone, and yet when it comes to love we are told rationality is unromantic. We are told that it's offensive to consider partnership through a practical and balanced lens, that this cheapens it. But this is just another way MOTO tries to take the wild complexity of love and partnership and reduce it down to a single bland flavor.

If we shouldn't rely on our feelings, then what should we trust? My clients ask this question a lot, an inquiry that reflects the emphasis that has been placed on emotions as our only guideposts to good love. Emotions matter, but so do other factors that must be taken into consideration. The answer is to look for good-enough levels when evaluating your relationship. For example, do you feel good-enough happy with them? Do you feel good-enough levels of joy, attraction, and alignment? Does your partner meet your needs a good-enough number of times? Do the two of you do a good-enough job at working through conflict and reestablishing connection?

If this all sounds like I'm advocating for you to settle in your relationships, then you've heard me clearly. I am. I'm asking you to settle from an impossible standard of perfection, the very standard that has caused you all the pain you're currently experiencing, the one that fuels your ROCD. I'm asking you to settle for the truth of what healthy love and partnership can provide, and to accept what they can never and were never meant to. Settling may seem like a bad word, one that MOTO has made taboo. But the curse many of us face today is not that we settle for a bad partner, but that we never feel settled at all. We refuse to accept anything less than perfect.

While we're on the topic of undoing and unlearning...

## Don't Fall in Love

*Walk into it.* Resist the MOTO mandate that the only way love is legitimate is if it involves rushing in headlong. So often what I see in the treatment of ROCD and relationship anxiety are people who carry an incredible amount of shame around the way their relationship started. They feel that their love story is less legitimate than others because rather than falling straight into love, they acted cautiously: they walked in. They entered the waters slowly, looking for trust and safety before going deeper, and worried that their relationship wasn't strong enough to warrant diving in first. But walking into love is a no less legitimate way to enter, and for those who live with a sensitive amygdala, caution and a careful approach are built into who we are. Think about it, are you the type to fall for anything else? Would you spontaneously take a job or drop everything and skip town for three months on an adventure? If the answer is no, then why should you treat love any differently? Why would you expect yourself to fall into something as important as love when you could walk into it instead?

There is nothing to be ashamed of in walking into love, no matter what MOTO will have you believe. Only check that your slower pace is the result of an intentional choice and not avoidance, the by-product of fear and anxiety. If you have ROCD or have experienced an attachment injury from your early environments, entering into love and commitment might always feel a bit touchy. Knowing this is not a free pass to sit out on the adventure and avoid the vulnerability and growth a relationship offers; rather it is a completely understandable backstory that validates your choice to enter the water slowly, if you choose to do so at all. There is no wrong way to love and no wrong pace to move forward, as long as you remain transparent about where you're at and what you can offer to your partner (or potential partner). If your pace doesn't work for them, they are free to leave and are justified in doing so. But the best sort of partner for you will accept your pace. They'll see the effort and heart it takes to walk, even if there appears to be no fall.

## Don't Believe Divorce Is No Option

What happens, if even after all the effort and despite all your best intentions, things don't work out? After all, it takes two people to make a relationship work, so even if you are the picture of willingness, you can't sail this ship alone. What happens if you both realize that you're headed in different directions, that you want the life of adventure and mystery and they want to throw a ball in the suburbs?

We all want to read a book on relationships and be guaranteed success. But here's the truth: some relationships won't work out. Something or multiple somethings might get in the way, be it bad timing, unresolved trauma, or unwillingness to let go of MOTO and accept imperfection. The goal isn't to stay together no matter what. So what I'm about to say next may seem scary, but it is an important addition to your arsenal of ideas and tools: *divorce is an option.* If things truly aren't working out, you can choose to leave. What's more, you'll probably be just fine if you do.

It may seem like I'm denouncing the message of hope I've been peddling this entire book, but stay with me a moment. I'm not saying you should take the idea of divorce or separation lightly, but having the option might very well save your relationship. Here is one of the most distressing thoughts for someone with relationship anxiety: if you commit (and commit you must if you truly want to see whether the relationship can work), then you will be trapped. You avoid commitment and good love because you're so afraid you might end up unendurably miserable.

You worry you'll be unhappy and have no way out. You may believe, however unconsciously, that commitment is a one-way street with no exits and that you will be doomed if your relationship doesn't work out.

The good news is masked as bad news. Divorce is an option.

Anxiety will say you shouldn't even take the risk of love because it includes the possibility of pain. But I say, try anyway, and if things really end up as the horror story your mind has painted for you all along, then leave. You are not trapped or doomed to lovelessness in this life, so if things ever get as bad as your mind says they might, and they stay that way despite both of your best efforts, leave!

I'm not being cavalier about how difficult this would be. I know you would be crushed. You would be faced with judgment from others for your decision and most intensely from your own inner critic. It would be hard to separate the life you had built together and start all over. But if you had to do it, if you had tried everything in your power and spent years working on things to no avail, divorce is an option. What's more, you would probably end up just fine on the other side of it. I'm not in favor of running for the hills at the first sign of difficulty, and my work advocates the exact opposite. But knowing there's an exit route that you could survive might be all you need to take that all-important leap of faith into the unknown, the leap that holds no certainty except for a promise that it will challenge you to the edge of your tolerance, right before it transforms you.

## The Gift of the Unknown

At the beginning of this book, I said I'd never tell you if your partner was the right one for you, and that I could never promise anyone they'd chosen correctly or tell them their love would last. I promised, instead, that you would learn how to manage anxiety and fear so that you could make your own decision with clear eyes and a trusting heart. I promised that you would have a path forward and tools to help along the way, and that if you were committed to an entirely new outlook on what it means to love, you would find there was another road to walk along: a path less taken but no less magical, only less advertised.

For all the tools in this book, there is one thing our work together can never give you and no therapy, coach, preacher, or guru can offer. No one can show you how to escape the unknown; no one can provide perfect certainty. No spiritual journey will show you how to eliminate one of the most transformative and terrifying facts of being alive: we simply cannot know what the future will hold. The best approaches won't claim to give you control over what's to come. Instead, they work with the one thing we can control, our response to it: the willingness with which we embrace pain and uncertainty as we look out at the horizon line of our lives and wonder, *Will I be okay?*

To fully live and fully love, to fully heal from the pain of anxiety and ROCD, we must respond to life's most difficult questions by humbly conceding "I don't know the answer, and that's okay." We must learn to live with boxes unopened and questions unexplored in our minds and recognize that the itch to solve, fix, and organize these burning questions into neat piles of answers was the problem all along, not the questions themselves. We must lay down our weapons, whether out of exhaustion or experience, and look for a different way forward than the one that brought us here. It is from this place, a place that feels like giving up but is really letting go, that something extraordinary happens. Answering life's most fundamental questions by throwing up your hands and laughing "I just don't know!" might sound cavalier, but it's the answer of an explorer. It's the attitude of one who has accepted that life is a journey and that joy doesn't come from having all the cheat codes to the game.

Congratulations, you've been selected to play! In this game, there are many unknowns but also some things you can be sure of. You can be sure that, no matter how scared you feel as you set sail, your fear will eventually pass through like a bad storm if only you hold steady. You can be sure that when you find yourself moored and alone, frightened and lost, there is always a way out, as long as you're willing to explore both the outside world and the one inside you. You can be sure that the journey won't be exactly what you expected it to be, and that it will transform you. And you can be certain that the most profound moments of your life are yet to be felt on the other side of the horizon line.

The secret you must hold on to in the darkest of days is that your ROCD is more than just a horrible cross to bear: it is a lifelong education in managing discomfort. It is an acquaintance with pain that will tear you open while it teaches you everything you ever needed to know about living. If you can master this, almost nothing can take you down. So take a deep breath and let it in! Your anxiety will be hell, but it will also be your salvation.

You just have to let the pain wash through.

# Acknowledgments

The opportunity to write this book has been a dream come true, and I want to start by thanking the entire team at New Harbinger for taking a chance on me and allowing me the space to share my thoughts on a topic so personally and professionally close to my heart. And to my editors Ryan Buresh, Vicraj Gill, and Brady Kahn, who somehow managed to walk the fine line between giving me the safety to explore and the security to come home. It has been a pleasure raising this book with you. I hope she'll make us proud.

Thank you to J.M.R, with whom life is an endless adventure toward the horizon line. For the laughter and joy you inspire, for feeding me snacks, for talking me down off every cliff this process has driven me toward, and for being the reason why my words are filled with meaning and intention. We made it to the other side because you never let go of my hand. This one is for you, my love.

Thank you to M.N.A, the other great love of my life. For believing in me from the very beginning, for coloring my life in a thousand different shades of joy, and for walking with me through the darkness. Thank you for the insanely precious gift of your friendship. I'm so glad I tapped you on the shoulder that day at the fire drill, and I always will be.

Thank you to my parents, Farhad and Farzin, who immigrated to this country and are, in every sense of the words, a success story. Thank you for the ferocity of your love and the endlessness of your support. For nature, nurture, and everything in between. None of this would be possible without you.

And especially to Faye. For every walk you ever took with me on the phone outside your office, every cup of chai, and every dream we've shared about a future beneath the oaks. We'll be there together one day. I promise.

To all the thinkers, authors, mentors, and teachers, whose words have shaped me and whose influence lives in these pages. And to my therapist Heather, for more than a decade of work together, for keeping me sane and being the inspiration for a career I love so much. I owe so much to you.

And lastly, to every client I have ever worked with. You are the reason I wrote this book, and to walk alongside you has been the greatest honor of my life. Thank you for sharing your stories with me and trusting me with your brilliant interiority. I know it seems like therapists do the teaching, but this couldn't be further from the truth. You have taught me everything I know about true courage.

# Resources

## Anxiety and OCD Treatment

American Association of Sexuality Educators, Counselors, and Therapists (find a certified sex educator in your region)

Anxiety and Depression Association of America (resources available to those struggling with depression and anxiety concurrently)

The International OCD Foundation (use their listing of psychotherapists who specialize in the treatment of OCD in your region)

OCD-UK (OCD education and resources in the United Kingdom)

Psychology Today (use their therapist look-up tool to find a clinician in your region)

## Books

*Attached: The New Science of Adult Attachment*, Amir Levine

*ACT with Love*, Russ Harris

*Come As You Are*, Emily Nagoski

*Mating in Captivity*, Esther Perel

*The Course of Love*, Alain De Botton

*The Happiness Trap*, Russ Harris

*The Imp of the Mind*, Lee Baer

*The Wild Edge of Sorrow*, Francis Weller

*The Wisdom of Anxiety*, Sheryl Paul

## Support

Intrusive Thoughts Inc. (mental health advocacy and support)

OCD Peers (online support groups across the United States)

OCD SoCal (Southern California OCD resources)

Peace of Mind Foundation, Inc. (education for OCD sufferers and their families)

The OCD Stories (podcast)

# References

Adolphs, R., D. Tranel, H. Damasio, and A. Damasio. 1994. "Impaired Recognition of Emotion in Facial Expressions Following Bilateral Damage to the Human Amygdala." *Nature* 372 (6507): 669–72.

Ainsworth, M. D. S. 1978. *Patterns of Attachment: A Psychological Study of the Strange Situation*. Hillsdale, NJ: Lawrence Erlbaum Associates.

American Psychiatric Association. 2013. *Diagnostic and Statistical Manual of Mental Disorders (DSM-V)*. 5th ed. Washington, DC: American Psychiatric Association.

Bancroft, J., C. A. Graham, E. Janssen, and S. A. Sanders. 2009. "The Dual Control Model: Current Status and Future Directions." *Journal of Sex Research* 46 (2–3): 121–42.

Cisler, J. M., B. O. Olatunji, J. M. Lohr, and N. L. Williams. 2009. "Attentional Bias Differences Between Fear and Disgust: Implications for the Role of Disgust in Disgust-Related Anxiety Disorders." *Cognition and Emotion* 23 (4): 675–87.

Chödrön, P. 1997. *When Things Fall Apart: Heart Advice for Difficult Times*. Boston: Shambhala.

Coplan, J. D., S. Hodulik, S. J. Mathew, X. Mao, P. R. Hof, J. M. Gorman, and D. C. Shungu. 2012. "The Relationship Between Intelligence and Anxiety: An Association with Subcortical White Matter Metabolism." *Frontiers in Evolutionary Neuroscience* 3: 8. https://doi.org/10.3389/fnevo.2011.00008.

Doron, G. 2020. "Self-Vulnerabilities, Attachment and Obsessive Compulsive Disorder (OCD) Symptoms: Examining the Moderating Role of Attachment Security on Fear of Self." *Journal of Obsessive-Compulsive and Related Disorders* 27 (3): 100575.

Doron, G., and D. Derby. 2017. "Assessment and Treatment of Relationship-Related OCD Symptoms (ROCD): A Modular Approach." In *The Wiley Handbook of Obsessive Compulsive Disorders*, vol. 1, edited by J. S. Abramowitz, D. McKay, and E. A. Storch. Hoboken, NJ: John Wiley and Sons.

Doron, G., D. Derby, and O. S. Szepsenwol. 2014. "Relationship Obsessive Compulsive Disorder (ROCD): A Conceptual Framework." *Journal of Obsessive-Compulsive and Related Disorders* 3 (2): 169–80.

Doron, G., D. Derby, O. Szepsenwol, and D. Talmor. 2012. "Tainted Love: Exploring Relationship-Centered Obsessive Compulsive Symptoms in Two Non-Clinical Cohorts." *Journal of Obsessive-Compulsive and Related Disorders* 1 (1): 16–24.

Doron, G., R. Moulding, M. Nedeljkovic, M. Kyrios, M. Mikulincer, and D. Sar-El. 2012. "Adult Attachment Insecurities Are Associated with Obsessive Compulsive Disorder." *Psychology and Psychotherapy* 85 (2): 163–78.

Eddy, K. T., L. Dutra, R. Bradley, and D. Westen. 2004. "A Multidimensional Meta-Analysis of Psychotherapy and Pharmacotherapy for Obsessive-Compulsive Disorder." *Clinical Psychology Review* 24 (8): 1011–30.

Fraley, R. C., M. E. Heffernan, A. M. Vicary, and C. C. Brumbaugh. 2011. "The Experiences in Close Relationships—Relationship Structures Questionnaire: A Method for Assessing Attachment Orientations Across Relationships." *Psychological Assessment* 23 (3): 615–25.

Gilovich, T., V. H. Medvec, and K. Savitsky, K. 2000. "The Spotlight Effect in Social Judgment: An Egocentric Bias in Estimates of the Salience of One's Own Actions and Appearance." *Journal of Personality and Social Psychology.* 78 (2): 211–22.

Goossens, L., S. Sunaert, R. Peeters, E. Griez, and K. Schruers. 2007. "Amygdala Hyperfunction in Phobic Fear Normalizes After Exposure." *Biological Psychiatry* 62 (10): 1119–25.

Gottman, J. M., and J. S. Gottman. 2008. "Gottman Method Couple Therapy." In *Clinical Handbook of Couple Therapy*, 4th ed, edited by A. S. Gurman. New York: The Guilford Press.

Gottman, J. M., and N. Silver. 1999. *The Seven Principles for Making Marriage Work*. New York: Three Rivers Press.

Harris, R. 2009. *ACT with Love: Stop Struggling, Reconcile Differences, and Strengthen Your Relationship with Acceptance and Commitment Therapy*. Oakland, CA: New Harbinger.

Hazan, C., and P. R. Shaver. 1994. "Attachment as an Organizational Framework for Research on Close Relationships." *Psychological Inquiry* 5 (1): 1–22.

Hicks, T. V., and H. Leitenberg. 2001. "Sexual Fantasies About One's Partner Versus Someone Else: Gender Differences in Incidence and Frequency." *Journal of Sex Research* 38 (1): 43–50.

Johnson, R. A. 1983. *We: Understanding the Psychology of Romantic Love*. New York: HarperCollins.

McNulty, J., L. Neff, and B. Karney. 2008. "Beyond Initial Attraction: Physical Attractiveness in Newlywed Marriage." *Journal of Family Psychology: JFP: Journal of the Division of Family Psychology of the American Psychological Association (Division 43)* 22 (1): 135–43.

Nagoski, E. 2015. *Come As You Are: The Surprising New Science That Will Transform Your Sex Life.* New York: Simon and Schuster.

Neff, K. 2011. *Self-Compassion: The Proven Power of Being Kind to Yourself.* New York: William Morrow.

Nestadt, G., M. Grados, and J. F. Samuels. 2010. "Genetics of Obsessive-Compulsive Disorder." *Psychiatric Clinics of North America* 33 (1): 141–58.

Perel, E. 2013. "The Secret to Desire in a Long-Term Relationship." Filmed February in New York. TED video, 18:16. https://www.ted.com/talks/esther_perel_the_secret_to_desire_in_a_long_term_relationship.

Regan, P. C., S. Lakhanpal, and C. Anguiano. 2012. "Relationship Outcomes in Indian-American Love-Based and Arranged Marriages." *Psychological Reports* 110 (3): 915–24.

Schnarch, D. 1997. *Passionate Marriage: Love, Sex, and Intimacy in Emotionally Committed Relationships.* New York: W. W. Norton.

Seabrook, A. 2008. "Hester Prynn: Sinner, Victim, Object, Winner." *All Things Considered,* March 2. National Public Radio. https://www.npr.org/transcripts/87805369.

Stavrova, O. 2019. "Having a Happy Spouse Is Associated with Lowered Risk of Mortality." *Psychological Science* 30 (5): 798–803.

Taylor, J. B. 2009. *My Stroke of Insight: A Brain Scientist's Personal Journey.* New York: New American Library.

Tennov, D. 1979. *Love and Limerence: The Experience of Being in Love.* New York: Stein and Day.

Ward, L., S. Erickson, J. Lippman, and S. Giaccardi. 2016. "Sexual Media Content and Effects." In *Oxford Research Encyclopedia of Communication.* Oxford University Press.

Weller, F. 2015. *The Wild Edge of Sorrow: Rituals of Renewal and the Sacred Work of Grief.* Berkeley, CA: North Atlantic Books.

World Health Organization. 2017. *Depression and Other Common Mental Disorders: Global Health Estimates* (No. WHO/MSD/MER/2017.2). Geneva: World Health Organization.

Yong, E., 2010. "Meet the Woman Without Fear." *Discover,* December 16. https://www.discovermagazine.com/mind/meet-the-woman-without-fear.

# MORE BOOKS from
# NEW HARBINGER PUBLICATIONS

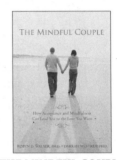
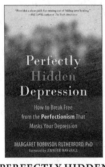

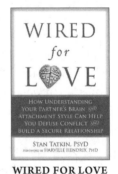

**Sheva Rajaee, MFT,** is founder and director of The Center for Anxiety and OCD in Irvine, CA, where she manages a team of clinicians specializing in the treatment of anxiety disorders and obsessive-compulsive disorder (OCD). She is a member of the California Association of Marriage and Family Therapists (CAMFT) and the International OCD Foundation (IOCDF). She has spoken about her own OCD journey in a 2017 TEDxUCLA Talk. She has appeared on CNN, been interviewed in *HuffPost*, and has been featured on multiple episodes of *The OCD Stories* podcast and other anxiety and mental health podcasts.

## Did you know there are **free tools** you can download for this book?

Free tools are things like **worksheets, guided meditation exercises**, and more that will help you get the most out of your book.

You can download free tools for this book—whether you bought or borrowed it, in any format, from any source—from the New Harbinger website. All you need is a NewHarbinger.com account. Just use the URL provided in this book to view the free tools that are available for it. Then, click on the "download" button for the free tool you want, and follow the prompts that appear to log in to your NewHarbinger.com account and download the material.

You can also save the free tools for this book to your **Free Tools Library** so you can access them again anytime, just by logging in to your account! Just look for this button on the book's free tools page.

**+ Save this to my free tools library**

If you need help accessing or downloading free tools, visit **newharbinger.com/faq** or contact us at **customerservice@newharbinger.com**.